MINIMALIST BUDGET

Smart Money Management Strategies
to Save Money, Debt Free and
Spending Less

TABLE OF CONTENT

Furthermore, the transmission, duplication, or reproduction of any of the following work including specific information will be considered an illegal act irrespective of if it is done electronically or in print. This extends to creating a secondary or tertiary copy of the work or a recorded copy and is only allowed with the express written consent from the Publisher. All additional right reserved. The information in the following pages is broadly considered a truthful and accurate account of facts and as such, any inattention, use, or misuse of the information in question by the reader will render any resulting actions solely under their purview. There are no scenarios in which the publisher or the original author of this work can be in any fashion deemed liable for any hardship or damages that may befall them after undertaking information described herein.

Additionally, the information in the following pages is intended only for informational purposes and should thus be thought of as universal. As befitting its nature, it is presented without assurance regarding its prolonged validity or interim quality. Trademarks that are mentioned are done without written consent and can in no way be considered an endorsement from the trademark holder.

INTRODUCTION

Has finances has long gone off beam? Where the heck did your money go?

You are no longer by me. Minimalist finances will assist you in showing your bloated prices right into properly-toned investments, spending on precisely what you want and not anything else.

This Book affords answers for the way we can use smart money control techniques to keep cash, Debt-free, and Spending much less.

This is not a get wealthy brief book. However, I can promise day-via-day, month-by-month, you'll finances higher and end up more precious as a result. Irrespective of how an awful lot your profits are, we'll discover a manner to funds, keep, and increase your Internet worth.

In case you're uninterested in the false and not possible-to-follow guarantees of "finance gurus," strive out my natural, honest, easy-to-stick-to techniques.

Enhance your spending conduct:

• incorporate minimalism into your price range

• a way to keep away from becoming a minimalist consumerist

• study the mental traps that make you overspend

• control your compulsive spending behavior

Feel financially comfortable every day:

• find out about two A-Z budgeting methods and the way to lead them to work for you

• learn ratio-based budgeting and fixed-quantity budgeting

• discover the satisfactory budgeting software packages

• design a bulletproof financial savings method to get out of debt, be organized for emergencies, and set you up for retirement

Forestall hating your economic life:

• discover ways to set smart economic dreams

• increase your self-self-assurance with budgeting

Financial training isn't a part of our instructional gadget. It's far every day that we don't realize a way to price range while we step into the craziness we call maturity. But it is not every day to live ignorant about an area of lifestyles that (find it irresistible or now not) ensures our fabric survival.

Money management is an essential talent for everyone who earns shops or consumes.

In case you follow the budgeting pointers on this book, you'll be capable of hold the song of your budget. You'll recognize in which your cash goes, in which it comes from, and wherein you can keep. You received experience harassed of running out of money; you'll clear yourself out of money owed and feature financial savings for higher costs like a vacation, new vehicle, or sudden events.

CHAPTER 1
MINIMALIST BUDGET

Minimalism doesn't sacrifice best for amount, in any case, so if you had to replace a vacuum cleaner, it'd be nice to spend money on a more excellent durable but pricier one (as opposed to a less expensive version with negative reviews).

That stated, it's also feasible to spend less with a minimalist budget—and in many cases, It is precisely what happens. Why? It manner of budgeting encourages frugality.

Budgets get an awful wrap. Not great sentiments that I hear are that they're difficult to maintain, impossible to stick to, and facilitate an attitude of scarcity.

Those sentiments are erroneous. What they imply is that how they budget or the price range itself isn't operating. A budget is a tool, and there are many approaches you can use a weapon incorrectly or inefficiently.

I was 25 once I made my first budget. I had over $50,000 of debt. I used to be making about $40,000. I had a new girlfriend I used to be spending plenty of cash on to affect. I had no concept of money control.

While my girlfriend paid off her scholar loans in less than two-and-a-half of years (of which six months she became unemployed), I requested her how she did it. She informed me she had a price range. I asked to peer hers, and from then on, I always used one.

Because of my price range, I have done a few economic milestones:

Paid off my debt in only over two and a half years

Saved the equivalent of five months' well worth of charges

Invested hundreds into a brokerage account

Bought an engagement ring

Finance has two functions: to make you mindful of your spending and to make sure you stay within described barriers. If we had been looking at a spectrum, some distance left could be "excessive deprivation," and the long way right might be "reckless over-intake." The trick is to live inside the center.

And so it begs the question: how does someone make excellent finances? My subjective definition of "proper" is that it's simple, clarifying, and as frictionless as feasible. All three attributes ought to exist, so one can assure an excessive achievement charge (as measured via how lengthy you keep on with it).

I've experimented lots with a way to make an excellent budget. Here are the first-rate three that I hold coming lower back to, especially after I genuinely don't experience like using one anymore.

Approaches   to   make   it   work

In case you ever wanted motivation for minimalism, try transferring six times in five years. As a pupil and now, graduate student, each degree necessitated any other pass. From more than one journeys, cars, boxes, and rental vehicles, there were expenses to choosing up and going someplace else. Hundreds of greenbacks have spent.

Every time, I enlisted buddies and family to fill up trailers full of stuff — maximum of which I hadn't used or checked out in months or years. All that junk fee cash and placed a burden on the ones around me.

It unexpectedly has become clean: having higher intended spending more. I was uninterested in the purchase of products that might need to be bought or lugged along. I felt dragged down by way of their literal and figurative weight.

With It dissatisfaction in thoughts, I decided to pare down my assets and promote the extra. Because of these efforts, my recent circulate turned into a cinch.

I packed the whole thing up into one coupe, with room for my brother in the passenger seat. I felt unfastened, knowing everything fit into one automobile. My entire existence was condensed. I was portable. That's after I embraced minimalism.

Existence becomes less severe with much less, and my pockets changed into satisfied, too. I discovered a satisfied domestic at the intersection of frugality, minimalism, and comfortable dwelling.

The Minimalist price range

Minimalism doesn't necessarily imply spending less. I may want to spend tens of thousands of greenbacks on some, select items. Perhaps I should purchase a proper gold table? For the ones maintaining close, remember, that would be one object.

There's hardly a restriction to lavishness that could nevertheless qualify as minimalism. The listing can pass on and on, but the message has to be clean: minimalism can lead to purchases that don't result in more fit pockets.

Just due to the fact you've got much less doesn't imply you're saving cash.

Stability among minimalism and frugality is the simplest way to pursue a life of less stuff at the same time as still saving money. Luckily, minimalism encourages thrift.

While we lessen wardrobes, electronics, area, and tchotchkes, we honestly see what we own— the consequences of beyond spending choices. Slight variations, adjustments, and additions have become apparent.

Put another manner, when we go down the grocery aisle for toothpaste, we're bombarded with alternatives. The alternatives span from pinnacle to backside, left to proper. Boxes put it on the market whitening, colorings, and flavors.

The beauty of minimalism is that it facilitates you note what you have and potentially reduce the urge to add more.

Conspicuous consumption tends to be a conservative approach to pleasing temporary goals. If we can get attention on some strength inside minimalism, we can become proactive customers—now not just customers.

The Power of a Minimalist Budget

Here are five essential techniques for recognizing the energy of a minimalist budget and the way it may have a high-quality effect for your financial savings.

1. <u>Give attention to lasting goods, now not all-in-ones</u>

Avoid buying gadgets that purpose to update other items. Those gadgets tend to fail higher effortlessly, and if one element goes, you're stuck purchasing any other object.

Even as all-in-one devices can store areas, they tend to feature expenses and failure charges boom. For example, multi-gear are more luxurious and much less reliable than standalone. We need long-term fees and excellent purchases that could stand the check of time.

2. Use your philosophy of minimalism to bypass preference

Minimalism doesn't work without severely inspecting what you want and how it'll occupy the area. At the same time, as the philosophy necessitates less stuff, it doesn't imply much less highly-priced thing. That hole separates frugality from minimalism.

The key is to harness the choice for minimalism to keep away from purchasing reports and apprehend that every new purchase will absorb the area. When we crave cloth goods, our biological brains are attempting to override us— tricking us into questioning us "want" more stuff.

But with the aid of reflecting on what firstly led us to minimalism, we will reassert our values and keep away from excess. Treat minimalism as a proactive, preventative force that enables you to avoid spending more.

3. Smooth and tidy regularly

When garments and fixtures dominate our senses and environment, we lose the capability to appreciate and understand what we already have. Vacuum, wipe, clear, and trash something you could with regularity.

4. Take inventory, compare want, and donate the rest

As you smooth, think about what you need and compare what an item brings to you. If there's a t-shirt, It is hardly ever worn, and perhaps it's time to donate.

Are there footwear or electronics that have been tucked away for a rainy day? How regularly do you watch you'll use that object? What price does it provide in your existence? And if it facilitates encourage you, donations can help you receive a tax damage too.

5. Create a minimum budget

Material minimalism is what most of the people consciousness on. They generally tend to love open walls and flooring. There ought to be room to think and breathe without litter. However, minimalism can be implemented in our budgets, too.

A minimum budget consists of fewer line items, with substantial budgetary cuts to make do with much less. The same benefits from decreased physical goods are present while dwelling on less.

Ways Minimalism can help your finances

Minimalism is a motion that makes a specialty of decreasing the clutter on your lifestyles both in bodily items and in other distractions. Folks that include it locate ways to take away the distractions from their lives, and it opens up more opportunities for them in different methods and regions. Embracing minimalism does now not mean that you forestall spending cash, but it can imply which you spend it on different things. Your attention can also alternate from earning profits to enjoying lifestyles. Right here are ten methods minimalism can help your finances.

Allows You to Prioritize Your Spending

Minimalism encourages you to embrace the matters which are most important to you. If you are not focused on acquiring positive gadgets, however extra targeted on unique reports, the way you spend your money modifications. Knowing what most essential to you may assists together with your spending priorities, and It could deliver ahead into the way that you handle your cash standard.

<u>You want less Room</u> (keep on loan or lease) While you are training minimalism, you want much less room to store the whole lot, which you have accumulated over time. While you buy or lease a smaller space, you may save on rent; however, you may nevertheless have a charming home with smooth lines and an area that you love. As you start to clear out some of your matters, you may discover that you may shop money via transferring to a smaller space. Now not most effective will It save you to your rent or mortgage; however, it may save you on utilities and unfastened up even extra cash to spend on the things that are maximum important to you.

Gives you recognition with regards to financial goals and finances

Minimalism is a set practicing mindfulness in your life. It can be gain you as you begin budgeting and setting your monetary goals. Budgeting is a spending plan based on your current priorities. As you discover what's most vital to you, it turns into less difficult to determine while and how to spend your cash. It may also help you spot areas where you need to exchange the way you manage your money like the quantity that you pay in hobby each month on numerous loans.

One manner to simplify your price range is to focus on getting out of debt. Many human beings start by way of paying down their consumer debt and then choosing to handiest have a credit card to deal with emergencies. Getting rid of debt opens many doors and offers you the liberty to go away a process that you do now, not like or take off a yr to travel. If you do not have extra month-to-month payments, it is a good deal easier to explore and do the things which might be the maximum critical to you.

Recollect promoting objects as You lose yourself of Them

If you are starting to embody minimalism, you could encourage the gadgets you did not want or need. You can use It money to help you begin to clear up the financial clutter on your lifestyles, like your debt. The funds can also go to leap-begin an emergency fund or to fund a journey that you have always desired to take. As you rid yourself of the muddle to your lifestyles, you may use the money to remedy your financial mistakes too. Protecting a yard sale is a smooth manner to sell some objects quickly.

Helps you locate approaches to simplify your budget

There are several things you can do to make managing your budget less complicated. You can pay your payments all on someday. You may transfer to cash for everyday purchases, which makes tracking your spending less stressful. You can additionally need to discover an app that simplifies the budgeting process. If you find a cellular app that works for you, you could enter purchases on the go and now wherein you are with your dreams and boundaries.

<u>Makes Giving less complicated</u>

While you understand what is most vital and feature your budget below manipulate, it could make giving back more straightforward. It can imply giving back in time or giving returned through donations. While you are practicing minimalism, it is easy to apprehend what you can provide and how much you can deliver. It makes shifting your priorities less stressful while needed.

Is It Easier To Budget As A Minimalist?

On the subject of budgeting, no person budget is right for all and sundry. The important thing, for plenty, is determining wishes as opposed to needs or organizing a minimalist price range.

Make It Simple With A Minimalist Budget

A minimalist price range doesn't always mean you turn out to be the man or woman whose mattress is at the ground and refuses to buy anything new.

You base your budget on your desires and not anything else.

That could be an actual minimalist price range. It doesn't imply you want to cast off worldly possessions or even exchange your way of life, notably. Determine your wishes and construct your budget around that.

Determine your cash float. Before placing a price range, you'll want to recognize how tons of money you are bringing in (and from where). Ensure you most unaffected tally regular supply of profits – don't rely upon windfalls, instant cash, or bonuses.

What are your needs? After you've determined coins drift, you can take a seat down and make a list of your desires and what kind of the price. As MJ discusses within the video above, those are typically things like rent or your mortgage price, coverage, food, and different requirements. When you have children, It can also include daycare prices and other childcare-associated bills.

What is left over? Take your income, subtract your wishes, and what's leftover is what you have got left to spend on amusing, invest, and store.

What makes It budget minimalist is that there may be no leisure or unnecessary prices built into your finances. As an example, a few people might also finance around $four hundred for such things as date night, going out to dinner, or seeing a film. It budget allows for that (after your need are looked after); however, it isn't deliberate.

Minimalist finances and Budgeting

My fees

Allows communicate about absolute prices. These are genuinely the things I should pay to stay my modern lifestyle:

Hire (consists of trash and water)

Utilities (gasoline and electric powered)

Vehicle insurance (I don't have an automobile fee)

Gas (for what little I do power; I stroll when I will)

Food (along with tips; don't be a jerk, advice nicely)

Medical health insurance & scientific expenses

Cellphone (optionally available)

Health club (optional)

That's it. I didn't encompass totals due to the fact yours will be distinct. So plug within the numbers for yourself, and that's what you want to live. For me, those expenses don't depend on cash for things I want to do outdoor of my total costs, such situations as live shows or films or different occasions that require money. However, the ones matters are optionally available, and I don't need to do them. If I don't have the cash to do them, I don't. I can be content quietly sitting in a quiet room on my own.

A observe approximately medical insurance: if you need to leave your job or start your profitable business or are already self-employed, I still advocate having a few types of health insurance. Positive, some people don't have medical insurance, but there are options for non-company humans. The most not great alternatives are as follows:

Purchase high-deductible coverage

Check fees with the Freelancer's Union

Examine quotes with an coverage dealer

Get coverage through your spouse's agency

Pass to Massachusetts or take plenty of vitamins

A notice approximately your savings account: its miles important to have an emergency fund saved, which you don't contact. Rule of thumb is 3 to six months of simple living costs (food and refuge). Adam Baker indicates you a way to make money from promoting your crap; that's a remarkable manner to accumulate a few small savings.

Fees I removed

These are the expenses I used to have, however, bumped off (over a yr duration):

Residence charge (sold the house)

Home owner's insurance (bought the residence)

Automobile charge (paid off the auto)

Cable tv (bumped off my television)

Net (I'm going some other place for net)

New garments every month

Credit score card #1

Credit card #2

Credit card #three

Credit score card #4 (yes, I had four credit cards. No, I'm now not kidding. I still owe a little money on certainly one of them and plan to pay it off It year.)

Student loans (paid off)

Different miscellaneous debt (paid off)

Junk

Junk

Junk (yes, I used to buy a whole lot of trash, however, I'm now not buying that stuff anymore)

Trading cash For Freedom

One important I stay through is wondering all my purchases. It takes time to earn money, and my time is my freedom, so by using giving up my cash, I'm giving up small pieces of my freedom. Before I make a purchase (even for a cup of coffee), I say to myself, "is It cup of espresso worth $2 of my freedom?" It has significantly modified my mindset.

Income

Once people know how whole lot cash they need, they continually want to know how to make that a good deal cash on the way to go away their soul-crushing job or find a task that they enjoy higher that would pay less. These humans frequently say, "but I don't need to put in writing or start an internet site to make a dwelling." I mean, that's adequate! In case you begin a website like It one to create wealth, you will need probable fail. Yes, we make some cash from It website now; however, that's not why we started it. Yet that's not your passion besides, so...

First, you should pick out your passions. It one is simple for some humans, and you would possibly already know the answer. In case you do, that's wonderful.

However, if you don't understand the answer, Jonathan Mead does a stunning task explaining the keys to discovering your ardor.

What about you? What is your ardor? Do you want to start a profitable commercial enterprise? Do you need to teach kids? Do you need to begin a blog? Do you want to jot down a novel? Do you want to end up a scientist? Do you want to travel the world? Do you need to feed the homeless?

Second, you must perceive your undertaking in life. It one's a bit trickier or even a bit philosophical. Occasionally, in case you're very fortunate, your mission is the identical issue as your ardor; however, it's all proper if it's different, too (it's extraordinary for me).

Another manner of studying It is to invite you, "what is the meaning of my life?" Good enough, I'll admit, that is an incredibly complicated and esoteric query, so let's get rid of the complexities. Regardless of the answer's specificity, the answer always revolves around two things:

Private increase

Contributing to others
In different words, the means of my existence is to grow as an individual and make contributions to other people in a meaningful manner. And the freshest news is that you get to determine the way you're going to do each.

Increase.
I grow in numerous methods, maximum extensively:

Writing & reading strengthens my thoughts and my craftsmanship, and it also strengthens my relationships because we have thrilling topics to discuss.

Exercising increases my overall physical and mental fitness.

Relationships allow me to hook up with others to get new thoughts and examine more excellent about myself via conversation

Contribution.

I contribute to others in numerous methods too:

Charity & network Outreach

I donate my time to charitable businesses; I additionally prepare larger groups to participate in neighborhood network outreach events.

Training and Mentoring

I assist others while they're seeking out path

Writing. Brilliant writing uniquely contributes to readers: book can connect to some other individual on a level that different varieties of entertainment are incapable of doing

How about you? In what ways do you grow? In what ways do you contribute? How could you want to develop and add? Make a list and select your top three in every class. Awareness on the ones, they're your task.

Liberating yet Terrifying

After you do that—once you discover your ardor and task—it's eye establishing. It's liberating. But it's also terrifying.

It's freeing due to the fact the whole thing changes for you. You sense new and excited and unfastened. Now you have something to focus on, and your life has a cause, it has which means.

It's terrifying because you realize that the existence you've been residing has been total bullshit, you recognize which you must trade, because if you don't change then, you're lifeless.

What Does Minimalism Have To DO Together With Your Money?

You likely have heard of minimalism; however, you can now not understand what it has to do with money.

I am prioritizing what's precious to you, even as deliberately decreasing clutter in other areas. Yet as the general public focuses on DE cluttering fabric items after they undertake minimalism (assume cloth cabinet or domestic décor), minimalism may be followed in your economic lifestyles, too.

Associated: Minimalism, money, and My garments

A minimalist finances will give you readability along with your cash with the aid of DE cluttering your price range and prioritizing your financial desires.

One caveat I need to say here is that a minimalist price range doesn't always suggest you'll spend much less cash. You may simplify your budget even as nonetheless, spending a lot of money on a few objects.

Minimalism in and of itself will no longer lead to spending much less money. Study It submit approximately the difference among minimalism and frugal living to get higher information of what I'm talking around. The two principles are different. Very one-of-a-kind!

But, when you lessen confusion and clutter in your economic lifestyles, you'll emerge as acutely aware of how you're spending your cash. Will increase the likelihood that you'll at the least be very aware of excessive spending. And focus is the first step to trade.

I'm a lot greater minimalist than I'm frugal. I might instead have a few, high satisfactory items, then ten objects that I purchased on sale for lower fine. The equal is proper for my financial existence. I pick out to keep it secure and that makes my price range clean. I've one bank account, one financial savings account, and my retirement money owed (and I have o credit score playing cards because I've in no way had a credit score card).

What The Minimalist finances is not

The minimalist price range system won't save you the maximum bucks or make you the most frugal individual.

But, the minimalist budget will help you simplify your price range so that you have a more natural system that enables you to achieve your economic desires. It makes existence simpler!

I see It difference in my existence. I've by no means had a credit scorecard. It makes my existence first-rate easy. I don't spend extra than I've. I most effectively use my debit card (and I use it for the entirety). However, I give up at the perks, points, and offer that credit playing cards offer. I do that in the name of lowering muddle and temptation. It's ideal for me. I decide on fewer matters in the call of simplicity and price.

How to start A MINIMALIST budget

Now which you know what It minimalist budget is, here's a take a look at how you could enforce one yourself (and how I do it in my lifestyles, too).

1. Alternate your money mindset from borrowing/payments to proudly owning

Commonly, I pay attention to broke humans speak about proudly owning things in terms of fees. They'll say such things as "I purchased It vehicle due to the fact I got a notable deal at the rent – the bills are simplest $200 in keeping with month." The aim is to stretch their budget out as a long way as feasible, ensuring they have got the lowest payments, to be able to live past their method in a life-style they sense entitled to but can't have enough money.

The minimalist finances require you to flip It mentality upside-down. Instead of questioning in terms of bills, you want to suppose in phrases of possession. Don't ask what the month-to-month fee is, ask what the value is to buy the item outright.

How I do that:

- I don't have a credit card, I'm no longer frugal, and that I consider my earnings capability is countless. That is very distinctive from the majority's cash philosophies. After mastering approximately money over time, It is what I've followed and truly trust.

- Define your financial values and set up your financial priorities

To be able to reduce unnecessary matters out of your lifestyles, you want to realize what is extra to you.

It indicates you need to define what is essential – or precious – to you. Once what your values are, you can set up financial priorities.

Examples of monetary values:

Stay an unfastened debt life

Keep 20% of your profits

Have 30% of a buffer between your earnings and expenses

Donate 10% to your church

Retire at age 55

When you are clear about what your economic values are, you could set up your monetary priorities. Your financial preferences are mostly your economic desires. They're your plan from getting from wherein you are now to wherein you need to be. They'll range relying on your present-day monetary instances.

Examples of financial priorities are:

Repay all your debt in 3 years (credit score playing cards, scholar loans, auto loans, and so on.)
After all, debt is refunded, start saving 20% of your income
Begin donating 10% of your earnings to church now
Make 20% greater income with the aid of starting a side task (right here are forty-five ways to make extra cash)

Create an extended-term economic plan that permits you to retire at age 55

These are just examples. There are so many unique methods you could go along with growing your monetary priorities. If you are in a function where you genuinely don't recognize what your financial values are or what preferences to set, bear in mind the 50/20/30 finances.

Any other factor to recollect is the price of reviews compared to things. What the studies suggest is that you will be happier spending money on reports as compared to spending cash on things extra on that here.

It may experience like shopping for matters is the key to happiness (specifically in conventional, American tradition). However, that's now not actual. So fight it. And don't forget prioritizing stories over things.

It's outstanding duper important in which you set up your financial values and define the monetary priorities that allow you to create a minimalist price range. The foundation of minimalism is prioritizing what's important and forgetting the relaxation. To try It, you need to decide what's essential to you.

How I do It:

You may watch a YouTube video on my channel to get a glimpse at what my cash philosophy is and how I work to attract cash in my lifestyles.

- Create a list of your spending conduct and examine your intake

Create a list of all the things you put money into (examples include journeys to target, gifts on Amazon, wedding ceremony fees, travel, and any and everything in between). The extra unique you may make the listing, the higher.

As soon as you have written down a listing of your spending, evaluate each line object. Ask yourself if each line item is something significant for your life? Do you cost it? Does it serve your financial values and priorities?

Bear in mind, that by way of saying yes to one element, you are announcing no to every other. If you answer yes to something that doesn't serve you, you're pronouncing no to you.

Right here's an example. Let's say you spend $150 consistent with month for your hair. You'll ask yourself if spending $a hundred and fifty consistent with month is serving your financial values and priorities. If it's not helping your financial dreams, is it something that's extra essential to you than your monetary destiny? The solution can be sure. It can be no. The secret's to take into account that by spending money in a single place you cannot pay it in another. It's a distinctive way of looking at what you're spending.

In case you find that you're spending money on matters that don't suit in step with your economic values and priorities, then you have to cut these prices from your minimalist finances.

How I try It:

I keep on with my price range. I don't use a credit scorecard. And that I put on a neutral cloth wardrobe.

It constraint in my existence is so helpful for handling my cash and my spending.

- Simplify your accounts and credit cards

A minimalist finances are one which probably has one first checking account and one official savings account.

The bank account needs to use for all your discretionary (leisure) and non-discretionary (housing, debt, bills) charges. Your financial savings account should be used for your emergency fund.

Within the same way, most effectively have one credit score card (if you have to have a credit card in any respect). You'll be giving up some rewards, but you'll be simplifying your life and making it less complicated to be able to live prepared and on pinnacle of tracking your spending.

It is a vast place I see mistakes in. I see humans having 7+ checking and financial savings money owed – one for holidays, certainly one of taxes, certainly one of down price savings, certainly one of an emergency fund, and on and on. It's messy, and commonly, I see human beings borrowing from one account to fund the opposite. It's additionally something I see loads with people who are caught in price mode. They've bills going to several places, and they're saving anything slightly in multiple accounts.

How I try It

I have one checking account and one savings account. I have retirement bills, like a 401(okay) and a Rollover IRA, but the ones are necessary for my retirement financial savings. I don't have any new debts unfold out. It continues my finances super simple, makes saving smooth, and gives me readability and company. I absolutely can't consider having more than one debt all around the place (makes me crazy thinking about it)!

- Create a spending plan along with your income and costs

Even as It publish as an entire is a set developing a minimalist finances, It step is setlist out the unique line gadgets of your fees in opposition to your income. Within the other levels, I talked about simplifying, setting goals, and adopting a minimalist attitude. That is the step in which you want to break down your earnings and prices and decide in which you need each greenback to go (i.E., create your actual finances).

You could use my finances Spreadsheet package deal or create your personal.

An example of costs in secure, minimalist finances is:

- Hire/mortgage
- Utilities
- Groceries
- Transportation

- Personal Care
- Youngsters
- Travel
- Enjoyment
- Expert offerings
- Giving
- Miscellaneous

Whatever you make a decision on for your charges, remember that retaining it simple is fundamental to enforcing a minimalist finances.

How I try It:

I exploit my budget spreadsheets and replace them monthly (reviewing them weekly). I plan meticulously and keep tune with everything I'm spending.

- Automate your bills

Due to the fact minimalism embraces a simplified way of organizing your budget, it makes the experience that you must automate as lots of your payments underneath It finances.

Automate your savings (e.G., direct deposit into retirement money owed), debt payments (e.G., auto-debit your fee on the primary of the month), and bill pay.

The simpler you may make your price range below It finances, the better.

How I try It:

I vehicle pay the entirety. I make sure the automobile payment comes from my financial institution account, so I "push" the cash out (in place of the bills "pulling" them). It avoids other companies having my statistics. It makes life less complicated.

- Query all future purchases

Step 6 looks backward via comparing your past consumption, so you recognize what you've recurring spent cash on within the past.

It step is about thinking about all future purchases. With a minimalist budget, you ought to query all the purchases you make. Ask yourself if the purchase is essential.

Keep in mind it takes time to earn money, so each purchase you're making need to be worth the time you spent incomes the money.

For extra on reduces your prices, read the way to notably reduce Your costs.

- Schedule economic meetings to study your progress

It's one issue to get prepared and feature a plan – it's a particular issue to put in force it through the years. Things will change in your life to make you as soon as an ideal plan unworkable.

To review, examine, and revise your price range, so it continues operating for you, installation month-to-month economic meetings with yourself (and your partner if you have one). It may provide you with the risk to put into effect and exchange your price range as wanted.

How I do that:

Every Sunday night, I'm going over my budget and price range to make sure I'm on course and overview all my money owed. It's undoubtedly beneficial to have a set, weekly time for It.

How do You Budget like a Minimalist

All of us overcomplicate matters once in a while, especially to our budget. Whether or not you are a minimalist best now starting to study minimalism or need a less complicated way to get a manager for your budget, we ought to all take a few tips from minimalism to enhance the management of our money. Here are five pointers to finances like a minimalist and help you keep your financial existence in order!

1. GET clear about YOUR desires AND PRIORITIES

Make a listing of your economic dreams and priorities and keep it someplace safe. You want to make those goals non-negotiable.

Reference the list while you are trying to make a careful selection. It may assist give you a route and remind you what's crucial and what's insignificant to your money priorities.

With direction, you'll be capable of making economic picks plenty more accessible.

Extra time, these selections grow to be your cash conduct, and having control over your cash turns into a part of your ordinary life.

2. Get rid of DISTRACTIONS

In case you want to budget like a minimalist, you need to recognize while what and how you're interested in shopping for things you do now, not need.

Do you get an email publication selling a logo It is "your weak point"? Do you frequent blogs promoting merchandise you adore? What approximately brands you comply with on social media?

Cast off yourself from those lists, delete bills that poke at your buying temptations, and unfollow the influencers on social media.

If you can get them out of sight, they will be out of thoughts.

3. Remove DEBT

When you have debt, It debt, the objects tied to it, and your habits all own you. You need to hold THEM.

Discover ways to do away with your debt and take lower back control of your monetary lifestyles.

A minimalist would possibly eliminate their debt in one fell swoop or large chunks at a time.

Whatever the path, a new minimalist method to debt might be to put off that "clutter" as rapidly as possible and start curating a higher financial picture from there.

4. FREEZE SPENDING

It'd appear apparent, but It is the key to lowering your debt and saving cash. Simply. Prevent. Spending. Stop spending your money at the large cash drains. Those are usually the indulgences and impulse buys.

Find a month and make an aware selection to now not spend any money on the more discretionary objects in your budget for that month. You'll be amazed how a great deal of money is without a doubt leftover to save at the end of the month.

5. GET A BUDGETING technique

Most importantly, you have to pick out the budgeting approach that works for you.

My personal favored (of route!) is the Anti-price range. It's far the very best budget inside the globe, and it's simple too!

I love to think of it because of the minimalist's budgeting dream because of how easy, direct, and to-the-factor It budgeting technique is.

Anything you pick out, ensure you USE your budgeting technique regularly so you can see those consequences of an improved economic life.

A way to Get better budget With Minimalist Budgeting

Have you ever come to a point where you haven't any cash, notwithstanding receiving a huge paycheck only a week ago?

If you haven't, valid for you, I've. Time and time again, I questioned why I had a lot of junk; however, I didn't have sufficient for the necessities. I have come to pay attention to having other manner spending more, and in all honesty, I have been dwelling that manner.

I was making outstanding cash; however, I spent more than I earned.

Every time, I had to call on pals and circle of relatives to come and choose up trailers of stuff — most of which I hadn't used. All of that junk cost a lot and positioned a burden on my savings and those around me.

It soon has become clear to me that if I persevered on my path, I'd be eyeballs in debt.

One random day, I was browsing the internet once I got here throughout the phrase that stored me — Minimalist budgeting.

What is Minimalist Budgeting?

Minimalist budgeting simplifies your budget by way of assisting you to stick to what's vital and plan for destiny in the right direction.

It's miles assisting me stay a less stressful life while nevertheless having sufficient for the raining days and retirement. I call it 'the freedom lifestyles.' Minimalism has advanced no longer only my finances; however, also my bodily and mental health.

How I Do It

Assets and charges

To get a higher budget with minimalist budgeting, stick to simplicity as a lot as viable. In doing that, there may be one rule that I don't destroy: spend more than I make. It can appear so easy, but it is one of the maximum crucial things to paste. Think of it, while you spend higher than you make, you'd go into debt very quickly.

To make sure that your minimalist existence is a fulfillment, the primary thing to do is to decide what your month-to-month net take-home pay is. It is the actual quantity on your check or direct deposit after taxes. Then calculate your constant monthly charges. These are the ones things which you cannot avoid. For maximum families, it's miles:

- hire
- Utilities — gas, energy, water, garbage
- vehicle insurance

- fuel and vehicle renovation
- Groceries and consuming out
- health insurance and clinical costs
- cell cellphone and internet
- financial savings (retirement money owed like 401k, 403b, Roth IRA, and so forth.)
- youngsters, college and sports.

Some of these payments trade every month in terms of how a whole lot you have to spend. You will pay extra for your kids' school at the beginning of a faculty 12 months than inside the middle. Utility payments may also alternate too, that's why you'd do the calculations with the alternate.

For me, some of those charges are optionally available, and they can be used to be lesser or better. As an example, I walk every so often in preference to using my automobile — much less coins to be spent on gasoline.

You don't always need 'wishes' to live on or relaxed your future. A live performance, for example, is unique, maybe even enjoyable. If I don't have spare coins for that, though, I'll permit it to pass.

Every other aspect. Some people, especially new marketers, freelancers, and people approximately to go away their jobs, do not upload in medical insurance and a financial savings account. For medical health insurance, I suggest which you observe options for non-company humans, like the Freelancer's Union or your partner's employer.

Open a financial savings account that you don't touch, no matter how tempted you are. That is for emergency conditions and your retirement (destiny).

Real Budgeting

I mentioned above which you must spend less than you're making. Till you fix It part, every other factor will fail.

Through calculating how lots money you make month-to-month and what sort of (on a mean) which you, in reality, need to survive, you have got pushed ahead of your desires. Then, you'd comprehend that the entire past It is just a want, a number of that are extra.

I try to keep on with 50% at most going to essentials, and 20% at least have to go to my savings account. Then again, each person's profits are unique; however, make sure that your costs can come out of your earnings readily with leftover finance. The leftover is your discretionary profits.

To be more correct, take out your month-to-month constant price (as outlined above) out of your month-to-month income. The leftover is your actual month-to-month discretionary income. Your month-to-month discretionary profits are what you could spend on desires, like that gymnasium club, or underwater video camera. You could also decide to place it as more financial savings; it's as much as you.

Ensuring Minimalist Budgeting

After I to start with attempted the minimalist budget, I couldn't persist with it effectively till I took positive steps:

• I started the use of merely one credit card in preference to 3

• Stopped buying unnecessary junk

• only bought new clothes from my discretionary earnings or on no account

- I automate some of my bills and my financial savings
- go out for net when I can
- define what monetary cost is to me and my priorities
- sold a smaller house considering I didn't need to pay rent for a big area because of much less junk

That's for me. You could think about other methods to reduce your spending and stick to a simple and easy monetary plan.

Each time I'm interested in moving outdoor It, I consider how a whole lot of time I am inclined to paintings to benefit that cash lower back for important stuff. If I visit that golfing course, will I have to work higher to get lower back the less $one hundred? How a great deal of my time, strength, and freedom am I willing to surrender?

Rather than slaving at the table of increasingly more work, and being sad, I selected the happiness in simplicity.

Some other element that facilitates is reasserting your values. Thinking of what led you into minimalism may also keep away from your preference for you need. It can be a proactive, preventative pressure that enables you avoids spending more in case you allow it.

As you exercise It way of life, certain things grow to be less complicated. For instance, I am now out of scholar loan debt. Additionally, giving returned to my network in donations (and time) is simpler because my budget is under manipulate.

CHAPTER 2

HOW CAN A MINIMALIST SAVE MONEY

In case you've ever wondered how minimalism saves cash, then keep reading to examine more. I'm sharing the details of how minimalism advanced my economic existence and additional recommendations to help you live minimally and store cash too.

Does Minimalism shop cash?

Before we get started, I think it's important to say that minimalism doesn't mechanically save you money—especially in case your definition of minimalism is attentive on owning as few things as possible.

In any case, you may DE clutter your entire home overnight; however, It doesn't always imply which you'll exchange your spending habits.

It is why I'm no longer a massive fan of the "one in, one out" DE cluttering rule. In a feel, it offers you permission to preserve ingesting and spending, as long as you maintain DE is cluttering to balance the equation.

Additionally, I well knew that there are times while shopping for more fabulous makes higher sense from a monetary perspective.

It is because it teaches you to align your picks along with your non-public values and vision—and those selections encompass your spending habits. Let's take a better look at what It means in realistic phrases.

How Minimalism Saves money

Here are four practical approaches minimalism saves cash:

You become intentional together with your purchases
Decreased housing expenses due to downsizing
You have more time and energy
Minimalism encourages a protracted-time period awareness
Allows take a closer observe each of these.

YOU turn out to be INTENTIONAL together with your PURCHASES

For a maximum of my existence, I didn't position plenty of notions into my purchases. Instead, I asked, "Did I want it?" and "should I have the funds for it?" (and to be sincere, I wasn't even very strict with the answer to the second question ... if my credit card was not very successful out, then I ought to "manage to pay for" it).

I knew that I wasn't responsible, but at the equal time, I felt that so long as I didn't move into an excessive amount of debt, then my shopping wasn't doing lots of harm.

Then I became a minimalist, and my mindset changed.

As I DE cluttered my domestic, I commenced to regret spending money on so much useless stuff, and I started out searching at my things otherwise. My closet full of unworn attire becomes so much more than just a clutter problem—it was evidence of the hundreds of hours of my lifestyles that I had wasted.

Sure, I had traded away hours of my lifestyles operating in a process that made me depressing, to buy stuff that I didn't even really need. It became an eye fixed-opener, and I started to consider my purchases differently.

I began asking, "What value does It add to my existence?" and "What am I giving up in change for It?" earlier than spending cash, and with It attitude, I discovered that I didn't want to buy as a good deal anymore.

I discovered to prevent mindless buying because very few matters appeared worth the sacrifice of my treasured time, cash, and electricity.

Neutral colored sweaters and shirts on timber hangers
How many hours of your existence do you have to surrender to shop for these sweaters?
Lower HOUSING fees because of DOWNSIZING.

After DE cluttering my life, I used to be able to downsize from a -bedroom townhouse to a small studio condominium, which cut my living prices through extra than 75%.

Yes, you read that right—by way of more than 75%! I paid loads much less in rent, and my utilities have been substantially much less too. It's incredible the way it all added up.

I recognize It isn't feasible for all people, and to be sincere, it wasn't a protracted-term solution for me. (I now stay in a 660 square foot condo, that's much smaller than my townhome but almost three instances the scale of my studio rental).

Still, I particularly recommend that each person who is trying to store cash do not forget downsizing—even supposing it's just a brief solution.

Your hire or loan is probably certainly one of your most significant fees, so decreasing it for even a year or two can have a primary impact on your budget.

Even though you may downsize your private home, you'll possibly nevertheless find that proudly owning less useless stuff reduces your charges. You may pay much less on utilities, protection, or maybe storage.

You have got extra TIME AND strength

Have you ever noticed that on every occasion you're tired, busy, or overwhelmed, it's smooth to invest in highly-priced convenience purchases?

You purchase cast-off food due to the fact you're too worn-out to cook dinner, you buy milk at the overpriced nook shop due to the event you don't have time to visit the grocery store, or you deal with yourself to a rich coffee due to the fact you need a select-me-up?

I'm guilty of all of those due to the fact when I'm exhausted, and I am going into self-upkeep mode. I do something that will make life less stressful and that I'm considering my destiny or saving money. I need to get through to the stop of the day.

Fortuitously, because coming across minimalism, things have modified. Of path, I have awful days like everyone, but overall, one of the benefits of minimalism is that I have more time and electricity than ever.

It indicates I'm no longer seeking out short and clean purchases to assist me survive. As an alternative, I sense empowered to make conscious choices that align with my values and save me cash.

Minimalism Encourages An Extended-Time Period Awareness

While you DE clutter your home and existence, you begin questioning intentionally approximately what you're going to maintain and by way of extension, what type of life you want to create.

It encourages an extended-term attention that (as a minimum for me) didn't exist before minimalism. I realized that I wasn't powerless, and I didn't have to float alongside, doing what anyone else was doing if I didn't want to.

I didn't should be a slave to money; alternatively, I ought to use it to serve me.

I started to:
Priorities saving and paying myself first

Experience good about spending less

Reflect on consideration on my non-public imaginative and prescient and how my cash ought to assist me attain it

I learned how to get out of debt and shop some money by way of making small intentional alternatives every day to have more of what topics most to me.

I decided that I wanted time with my own family, opportunities to journey, and freedom to trade careers more than I wanted a closet complete of cut-price t-shirts and anything else I found at the clearance rack at goal.

Plant in a white pot, on white e-book, on a window ledge.

Minimalist dwelling hints with a purpose to prevent money.

Right here are seven minimalist living suggestions to prevent money:

Plan to save and do research in advance of time. The extra organized you're, the less probable you're to make impulse purchases.
Embody easy eating—learn the way I store money, lessen strain and spend much less time inside the kitchen.

If feasible, pick out extraordinary items to be able to ultimate over reasonably-priced "deals," so one can crumble after some makes use. (if you're on a decent budget, 2d-hand buying is a fantastic way to shop for first-rate items at low expenses.)

Know your spending triggers—what makes you want to save? Is it your way of managing pressure? Do you keep because you compare yourself with others? Once you pick out your spending triggers, you may make a plan to reduce them.

Work for your self-worth. Learn to resolve your fee as someone from the things you're personal. The higher assured you feel in yourself, the less you'll want "stuff" to make you experience higher.

How to simplify your lifestyles and save cash

In case you want to research more approximately how to stay sincerely and keep money, I invite you to download a free copy of conscious DE cluttering.

—

Conscious DE cluttering is a step-via-step DE cluttering manual and workbook wherein I percentage the precise process that helped me pass from shopaholic to minimalist.

Ways minimalist living will let you store cash

My closet on time changed into packed with shirts, attire, and sweaters — most of which I never even wore. I was out of hangers, and each laundry day felt like a recreation of Tetris seeking to set up each piece correctly in hopes that the door would ultimately near.

I was mainly of a hoarder while it got here to garments. Most of the T-shirts that used to crowd my drawers were from my middle school and high college tune days. After years of preventing to tame my ever-developing dresser, it was time for an exchange.

I spent the higher part of a weekend stuffing boxes and trash bags with vintage garments and hauling them off to the local YMCA. After it become all stated and achieved, I was surprised the difference, no longer just physically, but mentally. I hadn't realized the quantity of hysteria and mental clutter my garments had been inflicting me.

Cleaning out my closet caused DE cluttering my entire bedroom. From there, it turned into the bathroom, the kitchen, the residing room. The following issue I knew, I was cleaning out my entire house.

Several benefits have been immediate. I felt less stressed, higher at peace, and less consumed by way of the things I owned.

But, I had no concept of how plenty of an impact a minimalist way of life would have on other areas of my life.

What is a Minimalist dwelling?

The majority think of minimalism as paring down your wardrobe, living in a monochrome global of black furnishings and white partitions, and sporting the same style of garb every day. However, minimalism isn't really about DE cluttering at all.

In keeping with The Minimalists, "Minimalism is a device to rid you of lives extra in prefer of focusing on what's essential — so that you can discover happiness, fulfillment, and freedom."

In other words, the concept behind minimalist dwelling is to be extra intentional. It's approximately allowing areas for the matters that genuinely remember to you and doing away with those that don't upload fee on your lifestyles.

How Minimalist residing benefits your pockets

For the majority, minimalism begins out on a more superficial level — cleansing out the closet, DE cluttering the kitchen, downsizing to a smaller area.

What most don't realize is that the advantages of minimalist dwelling go away past having a smooth, clutter-free residence. One of the maximum rewarding aspects of minimalism is the fantastic effect it has on your bank account.

Value studies over things

Minimalism encourages you to cognizance of what's vital to you. While you forestall and consider it, you'll possibly realize that journeying, spending time with buddies and own family, and having new, fun studies are far higher value than living in a large residence or riding the most beautiful car.

Once you've got It cognizance, you're spending shifts. It's no longer a question of whether or not or no longer can you purchase those clothier footwear or that steeply-priced pair of jewelry. You'd instead continue saving in your next massive tour as an alternative.

Recognize desires Vs. Desires

The average American family spends over 90% in their annual earnings. A massive portion of that spending is going toward matters we don't need — as a minimum inside the quantities we eat — along with in-home amusement systems, eating out, and new garments.

Minimalist living allows you to identify what's crucial for your life and what's excessive. As a result, you'll start to recognize and cast off spending that doesn't align together with your values.

That's not to say you can't put money into the things you want. You'll have a clearer image of the needs that upload value to your lifestyles and the ones that don't — as an example, consuming out by myself because you don't want to prepare dinner versus having dinner with friends, or buying a brand new automobile versus saving up for a worldwide excursion.

Quality over Quantity

Earlier than minimalism, I was notoriously reasonably-priced. Fast style turned into my manner of existence, and I was continually looking for a high-quality deal on each purchase, even if it supposed sacrificing great.

Now that I've fewer matters in my life, everyone is extra vital than after I had higher. Buying fewer first items now not simplest decreases my waste; it also helps me save cash in the end.

For example, I used to buy $25 tennis shoes. While they regarded as a fantastic deal on time, they would spend the simplest closing six months to 12 months earlier than I had to update them. Now not to say, they weren't all that at ease, to begin.

The tennis shoes I have now fee five times as much as my old ones, however, they've already lasted six times longer, and they're a ways extra cozy on my feet.

Minimalist residing helps you view spending from a distinctive angle. Rather than getting the excellent deal today, it's about locating the product that meets your wishes and adds the maximum fee on your lifestyles. Extra regularly than not, It great over amount of attitude saves you money in the long run.

Fewer things approach less area

An obvious benefit of downsizing your assets is decreasing the quantity of space you want to maintain your stuff.

Additional garage aside, fewer assets additionally means less square photos wished in your private home. I'm no longer suggesting you move into a tiny residence, by any method. However, remember how a good deal cash you may doubtlessly shop by way of giving up even some hundred square toes.

While you most effectively own matters that add price for your life, you experience extra pressured to attend to them. As a result, they close longer, which means less money and time spent on retaining and replacing your belongings.

One example of It is laundry. I used to search for the cheapest clothes I may want to find. However, similar to the entirety else, less expensive garments usually manner lower-quality material. Often I purchased a new blouse to wash it once and see it changed into already fading or pilling.

Now, in place of spending $15 each for five different shirts, I regularly pay $80 or extra on a single blouse. In place of 50 reasonably-priced shirts, I've 5 to ten pleasant ones that I like.

I've observed It saves me cash in two methods. First, my garments remaining longer, and that in itself lowers the overall cost of updating and maintaining my cloth cabinet. On top of that, I spend loads much less time looking for new clothes. I can then use my extra time to work on other things, like growing my business or creating wealth with one in all my aspect hustles.

Pay off Debt faster

While you start to value experiences over possessions, understand your needs vs. Desires, and put money into fine over quantity, a natural byproduct is extra money to your financial institution account.

It is exceptionally accurate information if you're in debt. You can take all of the financial savings minimalist living gives you and use it to accelerate your debt payoff plan.

That may not sound just like the maximum thrilling issue to apply your extra money for, but consider the snowball impact. While you pay down your debt quicker, you shop on interest and cast off your month-to-month bills. Without the one's monthly commitments weighing down your bank account, you have less strain and extra freedom with your cash.

You also have the option to make investments a full-size portion of your earnings. The earlier you begin investing, and the more you need to invest, the higher you'll enjoy the consequences of compound interest.

Saving cash will become less complicated

You hardly ever even must strive. Without the compulsive need to spend, money begins to pile up on your financial institution account. You recognize your priorities and would instead store up for the subsequent grand enjoy or significant buy than blow your coins for immediate gratification.

Minimalist dwelling is more Than DE cluttering

After I first jumped onto the minimalism bandwagon, I had no clue what I used to be. For plenty of humans, me included, it starts with DE cluttering and downsizing. But, the mental, religious, and economic blessings are a massive, frequently surprising bonus.

First, you're DE cluttering the bedroom, and the next factor you already know you're making your last debt fee or saving up for your dream vacation. Minimalism has modified the whole lot for me, from my relationships to my cloth cabinet to the quantity of cash in my financial savings account.

Pointers to store cash

Even though the minimalist lifestyle isn't always just about saving money, it, in reality, allows us to create a better, tons more healthy dating with finances.

Minimalism is ready being very intentional with time and money we placed into different areas of our lives. Natural inability to control our finances well wreaks havoc at the thoughts. Once we learn how to be more intentional with our lives, it changes our dating with budget. One of the first steps in becoming a minimalist – is setting out very clean desires in our minds. As soon as we have that described, it's sure to sweep out the objects and areas our lives that aren't of priority and may be involved out without a whole lot disruption to the bigger photo. Minimalism is a dedication to living the quality of life within the most efficient and mentally healthy manner feasible.

The first steps into being intentional with spending behavior are to perceive the areas to your lifestyles wherein you don't experience entirely on top of things of your finances. To begin with, make sure you don't rush into absolutely changing your life-style, throwing half of what you own out as a way to observe the trendy YouTube specialists on a route to DE clutter your area. Take it slow to scan your mind for priorities, behavioral styles, fears, and resources of strain. Make a list of short term and long time dreams. Something lies out of doors of your list routinely turns into of decrease significance.

We should understand that a variety of our spending patterns are often visible using simple ordinary behavior. We don't even pay plenty of interest. Conduct is neither appropriate nor wrong as we generally act on them unconsciously, and you continually need to be aware of what you are doing. It's viable that It may be the most crucial obstacle in your way of turning into a minimalist. The arena is ruled with the aid of dependency. Our habits and no longer the environment or our circumstances make us into what we're. Matters in our lives are as they're only due to the fact we're used to It ordinary manner of residing. While we make even little tweaks to our behavior, the complete image will unavoidably start changing. It's miles the habitual, not the periodical behavior that impacts our existence most.

Right here are a number of the methods you may simplify your existence and reduce your expenses:

1. Downsize

One in every of the most significant elements of our costs is generally housing. General rule right here – you shouldn't be spending more significant than 50% of your income on housing. As a society, we got into the concept "the larger – the higher." We fill our houses with tons of useless things and add more rooms to keep It stuff. Do away with stuff that you don't use and downsize. We don't want extra bedrooms; we don't want higher large dwelling rooms. Clear the litter, use smart, functional layout thoughts and even small rooms may be homey and comfy, while organized well. You could regularly save $500-one thousand just using downsizing. When you have a further storage unit – cast off that.

2. Get a Roommate

It is an outstanding manner of no longer most effective lowering your housing costs, however, additionally preserving your agency. Loneliness is becoming increasingly more severe trouble in these days' society. Having a person to honestly chat with even just once an afternoon can make a significant-high-quality effect for your emotional fitness.

3. Take Public Transit and Carpool

Our next object on the list of most high costs is our car motorbike to work or take public transit to lessen your fuel spending. Carpool if viable.

4. Keep around for coverage alternatives

Store round to get better coverage costs. It's an enormous part of your month-to-month costs – well worth an effort to reduce It even a chunk.

5. Sell your vehicle

Scan your day by day routines and your priorities. Can you do it without a car? Will it appreciably affect your daily time table, lifestyle? If not – promote it. There are lots of automobile-sharing offerings to be had these days, which might be a superb alternative for you if public transit or carpooling doesn't completely cover your needs.

6.   Optimize   your   food   fees

Food is the following essential region of the subject. It's crucial as minimalist which you have your goals very clear on your thoughts. A few humans find the notion of cooking for themselves an assignment. Others revel in it; however, do so in a manner that doesn't embrace minimalism. There aren't any policies only – in case you experience cooking – embody it and supply It place of your existence more time. In case you aren't a massive fan – then simplify it, lessen the time you spend in It to minimum, even as still ensuring you're receiving all the vitamins your frame desires. Either way, you need to make sure your prices on It part of your life are very intentional.

7. Reduce ingesting out

It is often a big part of our spending. In my opinion – seeing buddies for a Friday night time dinner is a reasonable expense. However, buying your lunch every weekday isn't always – you can reduce that expense in half with the aid of cooking at domestic and not compromising in your social existence. Cut out espresso store charges; make your espresso if you enjoy it. If you could reduce your coffee intake – even better – transfer to water – you'll get better sleep and more healthy pores and skin.

8. Don't Be Manipulated approximately natural & Non-GMO

After doing some studies on natural vs. non-natural and GMO vs. non-GMO, I found out; I wouldn't lose a lot by the use of non-natural and GMO products. Particularly the latter. Non-GMO is a massive marketing promoting device, and not one of the researches to date has found any unfavorable outcomes to the surroundings or human fitness coming from non-GMO merchandise. The effects of organic vs. non-organic products are more arguable; however, it's no longer a definite "natural is better" result either. Do your studies and make your knowledgeable selection. Don't merely depend upon the marketing campaigns, and the ones are virtually no longer the source of unbiased statistics.

9. Batch cook dinner

It is one of the unique approaches to reduce your costs and time spent on cooking, even as not compromising on quality. Batch cooking reduces waste – consequently, notable financial savings. And you've got your food prepared for per week, so you rid yourself of the necessity to cook dinner for the week.

10. Prepare dinner only once an afternoon

It is a big-time and money saver for me. Whether it's from you frozen batch or freshly cooked – always make sure which you have sufficient dinner leftovers to your lunch the next day.

11. Consume the same factor For Breakfast each day

It will save a variety of money and quite a few headaches. I, in my view, consume oatmeal with berries and almonds every weekday. I don't have to have ten specific elements for breakfast, as I used to. Just oats, frozen seeds, almonds and cashew milk – that's all I need for my breakfast and the gorgeous element – it's one of the healthiest breakfast options you could give you. Weekends are a piece more democratic – I depart my options open, for the reason that it's a bit greater time.

12. Buy Frozen

Frozen fruit and greens store me quite a little money and time buying. Initially – you don't need to worry about them going awful so that you can have pair baggage of berries for your freezer, reducing the variety of your grocery shopping trips. In addition to that – it's way less costly than shopping for clean. You aren't dropping out on vitamins – do your studies here. Some websites say, which you might even get some advantages here. Fresh berries are selected before they're mature to allow transportation. But, frozen berries are picked in their ripe kingdom, therefore more nutrients.

13. Consolidate your pastimes

Once I started the minimalist lifestyle, I realized that I've three-4 interests, that fee me pretty a piece of money. On the equal time, seeking to find time for all of these pursuits, I frequently didn't spend enough time on everyone in every one of them to get real benefits. I caught to at least one interest best, which gave me much less clutter in my mind, less clutter in my rental and genuinely, reduced my costs.

14. Have a leisure budget

Even as going out to see your buddies is healthful and vital, you don't want to blow your month-to-month budget on movies and eating places. Make a price range and stick with it. Or discover much less high priced options – like inviting your buddies over. Films are abundant at the net, almost anything is available at your fingertips, and the gasoline, time and electricity stored through watching movies from domestic is significant. Cooking a beautiful meal for your friends at local might be a high-quality, less steeply-priced and, often, a good deal healthier alternative.

15. Get creative with entertainment alternatives

If you are willing to put in a touch bit of effort, you can store a whole lot of cash right here. First, perceive places which are in all likelihood to enchantment for your tastes and research while an occasion is taking vicinity that you would possibly experience. Song, theatre, dance, art shows, and social gatherings are all taking place, and all you need to do is locate the right retailers that promote these activities and plan hence. In preference to dancing on the membership, discover a meet-up institution, and perhaps someone is aware of someplace better that has a first-rate dancing atmosphere without spending a dime. The opportunities are countless with regards to entertainment. You have to be willing to assume outdoor the box and adjust your expectations on what being involved without a doubt is.

16. Reduce your expenses on health

Scan your health prices and see in case you genuinely use all your memberships to the max. If no longer – see if you can upgrade/downgrade your package at the health club, or find a less expensive alternative to your location. When I looked over my yoga studio attendance – I realized that if I upgraded to a massive package deal, I would store close to $3 in step with elegance – which got here to $24-30 per month. I saved without compromising on my fitness dreams.

17. Try free fitness alternatives

You usually ought not to have a flowery health club membership to stay healthy. Unfastened weights and calisthenics will take you just as ways like the ones fancy machines used to electrify new individuals. A pull-up bar, a few pushups and squats can all be done in the comfort of your house. Unfastened weights are extraordinarily inexpensive while offered used, so take a look at your nearby listings and try to accumulate a hard and fast. There's a plethora of terrific exercises you could do from home with just a few dumbbells and a chair. Check YouTube for an excellent permanent and start from there. At home workouts shop time and money, a homerun combination for the minimalist in education. Don't forget outdoors – there may be no scarcity of going for walks or hiking trails right free the doorstep. Working out is a necessity, but a health club is not.

18. Stop chasing today's Tech devices

Society is evolving. The times of consumerism and acquiring massive collections of every viable gadget are over. Human beings need to revel in lifestyles, not be down via it. Having plenty of stuff does not anything to your happiness; it's a pitfall to succumbing to the worst factors of your ego. You aren't attempting to electrify absolutely everyone with your contemporary high tech machine. You are trying to stay a fulfilled existence with the precious time you've got on It Earth. Launch the ego and embrace the experiences. That is the ultimate aim here.

19. Simplify Your Closet

Take a look in your closet. I guess there are dozens of items of garb that you infrequently put on, if at all. Having a streamlined cloth cabinet is critical to adopting the minimalist lifestyle. If you discover yourself shopping for useless gadgets ways too frequently and getting little to no use out of them, we've got positioned your hassle region. Not only do you need to prevent It addiction right away, but you could also sell a number of your unwanted gadgets on Craigslist, eBay, or FB market. It step is so critical to promoting a minimalist technique. As soon as you have got skilled selling unused gadgets, it will make you think two times about every destiny buy you ever make. No longer handiest will you don't forget how useful an object is; however, you may reflect on consideration on resale value as accurately.

20. Reduce your software payments

Any other region in which you may need maximum probable find additional financial savings is your month-to-month payments. Hire might be a set cost – but a few other month-to-month fees, like power, water, fuel, and cable, might not be. Take a 2nd take a look at your power invoice. In case you experience extreme climate conditions on your geographical area, probabilities are there are a few easy 'does it yourself" steps that may assist lower your bills. In the kitchen, ensure your fridge is at the maximum green settings. Update antique units. Within the laundry room, wash complete loads in bloodless water. Remove the lint from the dryer every time you operate it. Separate heavy fabrics from lighter ones and avoid over-drying. When it comes to air-con and heating, there are lots you could do to save money. Close the vents of unused rooms. Use humidifiers in your house. Dry air is harder to maintain a constant temperature. Maintain the temperature around sixty-eight levels in the wintertime and 78 levels within the summertime. Each degree over 68 degrees inside the iciness is an additional three% added for your invoice. Inside the spring, use your open home windows to preserve calm if at all feasible. Update air filters month-to-month. These small matters add up.

21. Cast off Subscriptions

Net is a cost that the general public can not do. But, you might reduce your property Wi-Fi and find a free Wi-Fi station round you either thru an espresso store or public library. In case you haven't executed so but – cut your cable. It is a costly and unnecessary option that the net can easily update. Take a look at your monthly subscriptions. Perhaps you need Netflix; however, can you do without Amazon and Hulu? Are you oversubscribed to too many streaming offerings? Check with your month-to-month bills and see what different corners you may cut when it comes to month-to-month expenses.

22.   Store   on   vacations

Vacations are one extravagance that without problems can be adjusted to satisfy a frugal minimalist way of life. Taking the more time to devise your excursion will bring about massive savings. One sudden course of saving cash is probably last-minute deals. Attempt to preserve your schedule open while you recognize you might be due for a holiday. Airlines, hotels, and cruises commonly shop the satisfactory sale for remaining minute offers. Occasionally the savings for last-minute deals amount to dollar values that no dedication to destiny planning can provide. Make an effort to shop at the lodge. Search for offers. Scoop up closing minute gives. It stuff could make a massive distinction. When on vacation, don't be afraid to convey your food and drink as correctly. A quick ride to Costco will cut out lots of extra spending while supplying you with the foods and drinks you already know you revel. That way, while it's time to have that mandatory best meal out – you'll have extra than earned it, and you may even recognize it additional.

MINIMALIST secrets TO SAVING cash

Many humans turn to minimalism so that you can save money, to interrupt negative habits, or honestly to refocus their lives on non-cloth pursuits. And they should, as it works.

Frugality used to be a great topic among young people. Saving money changed into– at one time– what humans in their 20s did. However, as I go searching, I do not see a lot of my peers saving their profits. A number of my friends took relatively high-paying jobs right out of university, and are deciding on to spend as they earn: a high-priced hand-to-mouth life-style. Different friends aren't making any cash at all; they're volunteering, interning, journeying, receiving provide money, or enrolled in graduate faculty. It appears that very few people are building a savings account, for one cause or some other.

In It particularly unpredictable season of life, saving money isn't any straightforward feat. Furthermore, a lot of it has looked like intense frugality: zealous couponing, stashing cash in unusual places or selecting to handiest purchase clearance objects. While you're running lengthy hours, busy with journey or volunteering, or swamped in Grad College, who has time for that? There's no question as to why these time-ingesting techniques of saving cash don't work for quite a few humans.

So what does it take to begin saving cash in significant methods? We need to start asking ourselves the right questions. Saving money isn't about changing the manner you spend money, however the way you understand your resources and desires. Transforming your angle on wealth and its purposes is the nearest factor to a magic bullet for saving cash.

Minimalism helps us to store money– so that we can spend money on what subjects maximum.

Mystery #1: I'm now not described using what I very own (or put on, eat, stay in, or drive). Cash is often spent, unnecessarily, on building a photo. Whether or not it's far apparel, vehicles, devices, or maybe meals, maintaining a photograph can be extraordinarily pricey. Looking closely at how we invest in things to exude a positive lifestyle is one way to start reducing fees and saving. Only due to the fact everyone at paintings buys a large latte earlier than pictures does not suggest you need to, as accurately. Once I have done with shopping my photo and becoming in, I'll start being able to put my time and resources in the direction of the matters that depend on me more.

Mystery #2: Ask not where the best deal is, however, where the best want is.

So many shops have us hooked on the idea that snagging a super deal is similar to saving cash. It's not. Now and again, a top-notch store provide will offer more than one item that you need. However, usually, it's greater approximately making you feel that you acquire the lengthy cease of the stick- for once!

Mystery #3: Minimalism maintains my values always in my mind. As soon as minimalism seeps into a couple of areas of my lifestyles, I much extra centered on what I preferred, envisions, worship, and love. My biggest lifestyle priorities are always on my thoughts, where they should be. I did not often do something without knowing why I'm doing it. Whether or not I get geared up in ten minutes, journeying to a new destination, or spending time exterior, minimalism facilitates me to live intentionally. And for that reason, I devote cash deliberately, no longer by chance.

Secret #4: Minimalism is the enemy of litter and busy-ness. The dedication to not accruing lots of stuff is at the center of minimalism. And the name of the game to avoiding stuff? Buying most effective what is needed, only once in a while in bulk, and most effective inside the maximum greenway. Promotions that offer a prize for spending $50 at a store not often entice me anymore. I not usually "buy one get one loose" until I want both applications of the same aspect. I do now not replace an object until it has completely wiped out; far not only long past out of favor. In the quest for owning much less and residing higher, we turn out to be much less at risk of accidental accumulations and impulse purchases.

Mystery #5: Minimalism rings a bell in my memory that contentment can never be sold, offered, or stolen.

Although we would recognize It to be proper, it is so hard to live out. It is one of the hardest truths that I have found out currently. When we make purchases, we often justify them by using the "satisfied points" that they merit. How many times have I stated, If I just had It, then I would be a lot better off.? However, in case you've spent some time trying to gather one higher factor to bring contentment, you may have located— like I did— that it doesn't make paintings. Peace is not at the shelves at target or in our digital online buying carts. Contentment is somewhere in the ones matters that rely most deeply to us: buddies, religion, passion, network, adventure... the issues that have no charge tag at all.

Excellent easy ways that Minimalism saves your money

Dwelling the minimalist lifestyle is a developing movement. Families and individuals everywhere in the international are starting to recognize and are available to an agreeance that lifestyles aren't approximately the number of greedy gadgets you very own, but roughly the memories that you make with your friends and own family.

Is it feasible to live with much less? Simply
No longer only can you simplify your life; however, minimalism will shop your family cash.

Here are three ways a minimalist lifestyle will help prevent cash!

1. You start to forget about the Joneses.

Getting caught up inside the concept technique that it's a "requirement" to hold up with the Joneses may be steeply-priced.

While deciding to live your existence as easy as viable, you learn how to stay more, with less — other stories, extra memories, and extra happiness.

When you simplify your life, you simplify your preference to hold up with the Joneses.

2. You begin the use of coins once more.

Residing minimum way which you use cash (or your available budget) to purchase your need to-want gadgets in preference to relying on credit cards to stay your each day life.

Wants and impulse purchases with credit playing cards are a concise way to overspend and bust the lowest line of your budget. Buying on credit score is one of the fastest approaches to throw away your tough-earned cash.

Say you operate your credit score card to buy something on sale. You're going to spend the cash that you just "saved" paying interest charges to the credit card organization. It's far a smooth entice to get stuck in, but we will all agree it makes no feel. Why give the credit card businesses your money by way of paying them a hobby?

Paying in cash for items that you genuinely want is a high-quality, straightforward manner to store money. When living a minimalist lifestyle, credit score playing cards speedy grow to be the enemy.

3. You start to comprehend the difference between needs and wants.

To achieve success for your journey, you need to apprehend what it will take to live within your way and needs. At the same time, as half of your frame and brain can also want you to have fun and impulse buy and spend money on your desires, the minimalist aspect of you begins to understand the difference among want and want. It could be a tricky line to balance but receives easier through the years.

Desires are critical; wishes are not a need. The faster you could reduce out that spending on those frivolous needs, the quicker you'll start saving money every month.

Dip your toe within the water of minimalist dwelling.

For the subsequent thirty days, try to minimize your desires and attention to your own family's wishes. Additionally, begin saving receipts on every buy your whole circle of relatives makes — groceries, gas, consuming out, items for birthday parties, medications, bills, the complete 9 yards.

At the cease of the month, pull out that stack receipts from your shoebox, wallet, and handbag and make a huge pile. Here comes the attention-establishing component ... you're going to have a look at where your cash went for the last month. Our circle of relatives used the loose Dave Ramsey budgeting device, every greenback, the first time we did It. I was much surprised by way of how a great deal we spent consuming out (which I'd have stated we by no means did in case you'd asked me), on one-off coffees, and additionally how a whole lot we spent on Amazon movies.

While you watch and recognize precisely in which your money goes, it evokes you to make changes. With the aid of cutting out the extra's in your existence and paying most effective the needed bills, your pocketbook will start to refill quickly with all of the money that you'll be saving.

The earlier that you could embody the whole thing that the minimalist way of life has to provide, the sooner that you'll begin residing an existence complete of ways to store cash and eliminate a number of the brought pressures and pressure of the arena!

Ways To Save Money With Minimalism

When I finished Grad College, I was a large number. In debt and disorganized, it looked like I used to be simply mountain climbing a mountain of issues and not using a result of insight. Fortunately, I, due to the fact, have determined minimalist dwelling. It's enabled me to shop cash and provide you with a focused attack on my debt. Allow me to stroll you through some of the ways that minimalism has helped me save that you could do, too!

Seven methods to save money with Minimalism

1.   <u>I   consolidated   my   pastimes.</u>
We stay in an age wherein just about every imaginable hobby or interest is at our fingertips. Not can we have to look ahead to our nearby theater to show our favorite play; we will catch movies at clearly any time in theaters, on our home DVD gamers, or over the net.

2. I consolidated my pantry

Much like my situation above, I had an ever-transferring interest in exclusive ingredients. I wasn't entirely on the factor wherein I used to be consuming ramen every night, but I honestly had to look at my meals finances. What I did that helped me the maximum changed into coming up with a meal prep plan. On Sunday, I organized a full set of food for lunch, and now and then dinner, for that week. The usage of reasonably-priced components such as rice or pasta and making flavorful and healthy dishes with a vast sort of veggies has saved me lots of money.

I also store lots through developing my supply of some highly-priced gadgets that I exploit pretty regularly. I utilize lots of basil for "salsa verde" plus pesto for pasta and masses of other Italian food. It used to fee me $4 for enough basil to get me via or three meals. Occasionally I wouldn't even use the whole field before the leaves had wilted, so it felt as also though I used to be overspending by using lots. Its spring, I planted my very own basil flowers in conjunction with some other herbs, and for about $10, I set to undergo the whole summertime.

3. I used fewer home equipment

Plenty of people I recognize have two or more fridges or freezers. A few saved a lot of frozen meals and such, that's nice, but others wanted space for a wide variety of cakes and snacks. My mother and father even stored two washer/dryer sets around just as it becomes a pain to transport things that heavy. I since have discovered that turned into a terrible flow in more methods than one. Now not handiest, do old home equipment take in space. Matters inclusive of vintage fridges may have chemical compounds in them, which could significantly harm the environment if not disposed of successfully.

4. I got a minimalist roommate

Like quite an excellent deal everybody, I had my percentage of roommates in university to assist save cash on housing. With each new roommate, although, got here a whole host of problems, yes, they all poster kids for the case for minimalist dwelling. I consider one roommate used to eat nearly nothing but delivery meals. Chinese language food, pizza, or a sandwich, he always paid way an excessive amount of for indeed each meal. Then he would go away his leftovers out all over the house, making It dependency both high priced and unsanitary.

I'm satisfied to say I've given that achieved loads higher and found a minimalist roommate. While the whole thing is clean and orderly, ninety-nine percent of the issues that I could have with a roommate disappears. By using doing It, I've stored some money on rent without all the problems.

5. I tried questioning smaller

For me, It step got here a bit later within the system and it makes me feel that it did. When I had a ton of kitchen gadgets, some too many hobbies and wasteful appliances, I convinced myself I wanted a significant rental to hold all of these items. The reality is that once I cleared up different aspects of my lifestyles, it turned into a natural step to move into a smaller (and less expensive) condo. It also had the surprising effect of retaining me sincere in my minimalism. Impulse purchases continually are checked by way of the thought, "Wait, do I've room for It?"

6. I was assumed cautious with buying on credit

I get it. A credit score card is tremendously convenient. I'm now not right here to inform you to do away with your card. I didn't dispose of mine, and there were times while, used efficiently, my credit card has been top-notch handy and beneficial.

Now, what I mean with the aid of "used correctly" is I tried being accountable each time I used it. So I used it simplest when I had to do so or when I might gain from a rewards application. I'm very cautious to preserve it some distance, a long way far away from the things that you should never purchase on credit score.

7. I changed my mind-set

All of the realistic recommendations in the world received assists you in case you don't undertake a terrific mindset. Nowadays, I strive that specialize in the coolest that I'm able to do for myself and others by using DE cluttering. My old condo had It excellent system in which you can go away gadgets that you not wanted or wished on a table inside the laundry room. I bumped off lots of litter in It manner and picked up some pleasant objects myself, which includes a beautiful set of plates that I'm nevertheless using.

From the out of doors, minimalist dwelling used to look to me like a form of a peculiar cult. People that may want to surrender the whole thing at the drop of a hat.

Practical methods Minimalism Saves money

If you've study approximately the minimalism lifestyle trend during the last several years, you may have heard roughly the time-saving blessings that come at the side of it. With fewer physical possessions, you have fewer matters to maintain and take care of, which lets in you more significant time.

It won't appear to be plenty at the beginning, but the ones small-time financial savings add as much as create a critical impact on your flexibility and available time on a day to day basis. Comparably, proudly owning much less and taking a minimalist approach to lifestyles, has a very impactful result in your economic savings as nicely.

Taking higher Care, retaining things longer

While you own fewer words, there's more incentive to take super care of those things so that they final longer. One of the fine (and most commonplace) examples of It is laundry: if all of your shirts can healthy on a single drying rack, it's an awful lot less complicated to bypass the dryer; as a consequence, save you wear and tear on those pieces of garb. If you have a couple of masses of outfit whenever you do laundry, it in all likelihood received be convenient to air dry maximum of what you have got.

Those styles of practice will let you take better care of the apparel you've got, and it'll make final tons longer (in spite of other common utilization) and save you from shopping for replacements too often. Minimalism makes It less complicated using decreasing the variety of factors and the amount of time it takes to take care of them.

Buying fewer, better satisfactory gadgets

It can appear counter-intuitive, but spending a touch extra to buy higher best devices that final longer is an excellent manner to not purest decrease waste, but keep cash over a long time. As cited above, when you have an exercise in vicinity that prolongs the lifespan of the things you own, you could spend more money on fewer, higher-high-quality matters.

Footwear is an exquisite instance of It, where higher beautiful dress shoes may be resolved or repaired, and less expensive footwear frequently aren't well worth solving. The upfront funding may cost a little more; however, it saves an incredible deal of cash over the longer term.

Journeying Lighter, Experiencing extra

Taking an experience to someplace you've by no means been before is an excellent way to have life-changing studies and increase your attitude of the world. There's so much to research just using present in an area that is probably barely outdoor your comfort zone-however to enjoy it, and you need to get there first.

Whether you're touring between U.S. States or abroad, nearly every airline now has fees for checked baggage, and those fees honestly add up to make the price ticket you obtain even pricier than you planned. It'd take a few trials and blunders; however, it's entirely possible to bring the whole thing you want for a week-lengthy experience (or higher) in a single, big backpack.

Even the most price range airways will remember It a "non-public item" and could help you deliver it on board for no extra charge. Not best does it save you cash up the front, but it also means you'll by no means must cope with checked baggage that gets lost through the airline.

With just a backpack, the temptation to shop for souvenirs reduced because you sincerely don't have room for them-you might be consciousness of taking photographs and making fantastic reminiscences to look returned on for years yet to come. It indicates your journey dollars get you also, whether or not it's extra stops in your trip or some more incredible meals alongside the manner.

Favoring the practical over the unique

Minimalism has a way of dropping unmarried-purpose items in exchange for flexible, useful tools and add-ons. There are dozens of products like banana slicers, avocado slicers, and strawberry stem removers to do a single undertaking. Sure, each of these matters would possibly make the character mission itself a bit faster due to such a particular application. Still, it's nothing that unmarried, comfortable kitchen knife couldn't reasonably handle.

Modern-day tradition is full of these single-motive gadgets that try to convince us we need a selected tool for every movement when, in fact, something easy will do the trick.

Minimalism facilitates you embody It mentality, and helps you be extra creative as you look for practical answers to one of a kind issues the use of the tools you already have. While your options are constrained, you get to put your creativity to work in how you remedy numerous demanding situations in day after day existence.

Much less food (And other) Waste

There's nothing like going to the grocery store, stocking up on meals for the week, most effective to find vintage, moldy piece of produce hidden inside the back of your fridge when rearranging your new purchases. Now not simplest is it pretty unpleasant, but it's a waste of cash and flawlessly right meals. In the united states, upwards of 133 billion kilos of food are wasted each year – that comes out to approximately 1,100 energy per American per day.

You could save extra money and do your part to waste much less food by way of retaining the best meals you need to be at any single time. Particularly when it comes to perishables, its plenty simpler to avoid spoilage if you don't have a refrigerator jam-filled with stuff where it's difficult to track what's, and the way lengthy matters have been, in there. Taking a minimalist method with shorter, however extra frequent trips to the grocery keep will help store a ton of cash for a yr.

These are only a few of the ways that having a minimalist lifestyle will help you store money and spend extra time doing what you, in reality, love. Whether or not it's extra cash to your financial savings account, paying off debt, or extending an extensive experience you have got arising, the opportunities are endless.

CHAPTER 3

HOW DO YOU SIMPLIFY BUDGET?

Do you want to reduce the pressure of getting to manage a price range? Simplifying your finances and your budget lets you get a bounce-start on your year. Permit's lessen a number of that stress today by taking an examine some approaches to simplify your price range.

Simplifying does now not mean deprivation or being reasonably-priced. Simplifying is frugality in the first-rate feel of the word – making sure your hard-earned money is getting used for essential and impactful things.

Here are the ten excellent methods you may simplify your budget to discover some more money to place towards your goals.

Proportion a price range:

We sat down and created our circle of relatives' finances collectively. It can have taken longer, but we both recognize wherein the cash goes and why.

Automate:

Even when we've hit a few first bumps It year, our payments and other necessities had been satisfied. Most banks and credit unions offer free invoice pay. Getting It finished will prevent late prices.

Reevaluate Your Cable:

Streaming services like SlingTV, Hulu, or Netflix can help you catch some of your favored indicates at a fragment of your cable bill. Need to keep the cable? Name your issuer and negotiate a higher charge.

Get smart approximately Smartphones:

I get it – smartphones are enormously handy. That doesn't mean you should be having a hefty bill for it. Progressive organizations like Republic Wireless or Ting can permit you to have your cake and eat it too. I have telephones with Republic, and I'm paying approximately $30/month.

Positioned a coupon on It:

I love to store online due to the fact I'm able to discover some solid offers. To sweeten the pot, I use offerings like Paribus, RetailmeNot, and Honey to seek coupons and promo codes. It takes seconds, and it may save me cash.

Plan your meals:

Take an hour once per week and plan your meals. It can save you huge bucks because you're not running back and forth to the store for gadgets you may have missed. Want greater savings? Make some of your food ahead of time.

Have fun cash:

Did I propose spending money to store? I agree with me, and you want It. It's like being on an honestly strict food regimen. You're going to rebellion, and most times, it'll be massive. It's higher to build sound finance than a perfect one.

Consolidate Your Debt:

If you're lugging around high-interest debt, it can be wise to look if you could consolidate or lower your fee. Talk for your bank or credit union to view if they could provide something. You can additionally use peer-to-peer creditors like Prosper and LendingClub to lessen your interest. Just don't forget It step is predictable to help your debt snowball or avalanche go similarly. Getting out of debt is fundamental for your long-time period monetary achievement.

Have money Dates:

Get out of the house while you overview your price range. No want to worry about every penny, and those check-ins are to peer how you're doing universal. Celebrate your wins and look to enhance when you have a setback.

Mind on simplifying your price range

Those are my pinnacle ten choices; however, there are a lot more out there. I'd love to hear from you – wherein do you observe you can simplify your budget?

Ways to Make Budgeting easier

That's one of the most common reasons why many human beings don't budget. They either don't apprehend what a budget is, or they without a doubt don't know how to effectively positioned one together.

We want to help you see that budgeting is plenty more straightforward than you would possibly have experienced. It's now not scary in any respect! Budgets don't ought to be about complicated formulas and tedious math. Just like many different elements of your existence, maintaining it simple usually works wonders.

Here are five basic, tested approaches to simplify your budget.

1. Make a schedule (and keep on with it!) At the same time, as you're making the budget a part of your month-to-month routine, why now not pick particular dates for different costs? Installation automobile drafts out of your checking account to pay bills, and buy your groceries on a hard and fast day each week or two times a month—preferably. At the same time, the children aren't round to inform you all about how amazing the new Chocolate King Crunch Sugar Bits cereal is!

2. Make it a team attempt.
If you're married, then it's critical to make sure your partner is on board and is aware of what's up with the finances.

Sit down once a month and have a budgeting talk. Make it amusing! Chow down on a number of your favorite drinks and snacks to help your awareness. The vital component right here is that you're both on the same web page. That exchange by me will make your existence—and your money—a lot less complicated to manipulate.

3. Anticipate the sudden.

You've got your month deliberate to a T; however, necessarily, something comes up. Maybe it's an unexpected invite to a birthday dinner or a workplace toddler-bathe present you've been want to assist. You need to participate; however, you left trying to fit birthday dinners into your grocery finances and infant showers into amusement. That's no longer going to paintings.

Create a buffer for your finances by putting a small amount apart for surprising prices at some point in the month. That manner, while something comes up, you may cowl it without doing away with cash you've already placed some other place within the budget. Keep music of costs that frequently emerge as in It price range category. Finally, you would possibly want to promote them to a permanent spot at the finances roster.

Four. Split your credit score playing cards.
The first aspect approximately a debit card? It comes immediately from your bank account. No intermediary is charging a 15% hobby.

No credit cards way no more payments to add to the price range, fewer headaches, and 0 worries about expenses and high-interest fees. Stick with using your debit card (and even coins!), and sell off those credit score cards like your ninth-grade boyfriend.

5. Put off the paper pile.
Maybe you have a stack of receipts you have been that means to track on your price range all month.

Clean ways To Simplify Your price range

Dealing with family price range can feel extraordinary through a minefield every so often. There's a lot conflicting statistics on how to finances well — now not to mention warnings that just one misstep could plunge you into debt. As a result, we often experience intimidated, careworn, or defeated earlier than even starting a price range inside the first area.

Categorize Your costs

No more extensive understanding where your cash is going is undoubtedly one of the most critical troubles finance blogger Donna Freedman sees when operating with non-public finance clients. It will be annoying, as you could understand you're going over-price range month after month.

"while you realize you've got enough cash to cope with all of your wishes and a number of your desires — plus those pesky emergencies — you could sleep thoroughly at night," Freedman says.

Calculate in round figures how lots you spend on gadgets like rent or loan, insurance, gasoline and automobile protection, groceries, cellphone and net, utilities, and different residing charges. It may take a touch time, as you look through debit and credit card purchases, and try and take into account coins costs; while you're over, however, you'll be able to see the way you spend your money every month effortlessly.

Maintain It in a spreadsheet and update your charges as soon as a month or area. You could speedy calculate the percentage of profits for each category with the 0.33 device underneath, making it even simpler to manipulate.

2. Simplify your gear

If you're preserving a necessary, cash-in, coins-out budget, you don't want an intensive app with in-depth reporting and complex functions. Suffering to discover ways to use or understand it'll deter you from using it in any respect — rendering it vain as you positioned your budget at the backburner. As a substitute, use one of It accessible equipment:

Simple Budgeting Calculator: Its fundamental calculator calls for easy pieces of facts: cash in and money out. When entered, you'll get a dollar amount that represents your overall financial savings or debt, in conjunction with the share which you saved or spent. Set an intention and use It calculator to peer if you hit it every month.

3. <u>Monthly Budget Planner: Taking it merely</u> one step further is that It on-line price range planner that shows what number of your profits used for each class of spending. You'll also get a total for monthly fees, month-to-month profits, and earnings minus fees. It will assist you dial on your price range and get a feel for in which you can be saving extra and spending much less. Wallet: It is some other step up, but an essential tool for people who need to simplify their budgeting. Begin by using sincerely, including budget and spending categories and amounts. As you advantage extra self-assurance with the app, you could pass directly to putting economic goals, importing accounts, playing around with your price range forecast, and plenty more.

Three. Reduce Your quantity of Open financial institution money owed

Limiting your lively bills to a maximum of 4 will help keep you prepared and greater on top of things in which each dollar is going. Diversifying belongings is vital, but you don't need to unfold them out so much which you begin to experience crushed.

Take some time to consolidate into those primary money owed — checking, financial savings, emergency, and funding. The minimalist approach can lead to greater efficient cash control. If you have old accounts with a bank on your university or native land, however, use a distinctive financial institution now, near them and stay with just one.

Switch as many loans for your bank as possible as nicely (if the charges are correct) to make paying those down less challenging to manage.

Observe that organizing your debts isn't only a rely on easier management.

4. Manage coins with the "Envelope System."
Shopping in coins guarantees which you don't overspend — it's manner too smooth to swipe that credit card, in particular. At the same time, you're out with your significant difference or friends, which causes a finances imbalance.

To go cold turkey with credit playing cards, provide yourself a weekly spending allowance and take it out of the financial institution each Sunday nighttime. In case you run out, you couldn't get any extra coins till the following Sunday. You'll start questioning complicated approximately every purchase you're making if you could hold yourself to It.

If you don't want to go all-cash, designate a few classes where you tend to overspend, and use coins for the ones. For instance, It would be top for "play cash," like while going out with friends or on vacation. Put the allocated amount for each into separate envelopes that you could clutch while you head out of the residence.

Both methods help mitigate the danger for impulse buys even as you're out and about. Deposit any leftovers into financial savings or deal with yourself to something a laugh. While budgeting rewards you, you'll preserve doing it.

5. <u>Limit credit score cards</u>

There are numerous benefits to owning a credit score card, like income tour miles and the ease of having cash while you want it. However, having too many can quickly lead to overspending; as you max one, you flow onto the next. Earlier than you realize it, you owe more fabulous than you're making and get strapped with high-interest bills. That's in all likelihood why the total credit score card debt inside the United States is presently at $818 billion.

Even though the current economic system tends to operate on credit, ditching It exercise will prevent time, hassle, and cash in the long-run. Cut back on what number of credit playing cards you use, ideally keeping yourself to just one or two. Once you get your monthly payments and spending underneath manage, you may don't forget, including extra credit score cards as vital.

Start Budgeting

Taking the price of your price range can experience daunting, however, when you start the addiction of budgeting every month, you'll advantage the self-belief to start placing goals and planning for investments and security inside the destiny. Take into account: it ought not to be complicated. Understanding how much is coming in and what sort of goes out — together with wherein it's going — will assist set you up for budgeting achievement.

What are the Tips to Manage Money?

Cash control is a problematic challenge. For lots, the subject noticed a feeling of apprehension. Perhaps you've taken away saving for retirement for a chunk too lengthy. Or, maybe you're worried approximately no longer having an emergency financial savings cushion. Something your worries, perhaps, there's no time just like the present to get a handle on your price range. It's high-quality to get commenced – as quickly as possible – on excellent financial habits. Luckily, we have ten money control suggestions to get you started.

1. Understand your cash Priorities

Earlier than budgeting, you want to determine your priorities. If you skip It essential step, you received buy into your monetary plan.

Patrice Washington, a leading authority in personal finance, entrepreneurship, and extra, advises that cash priorities align along with your values. "the largest categories should replicate what matters most to you," whether or not you fee global tour or looking after your body. Then you could reduce again on other classes to "keep at most ability" on your real priorities.

Perhaps it's a wedding or a vacation you need to shop for or, possibly, you need to set up an emergency fund so that you're now not "up a creek without a paddle." At the same time, your car wishes an engine overhaul, or your puppy desires surgical operation.

Anything worries you most; make that your priority, as a minimum to start.

2. Determine Your Monthly Pay

As the pronouncing is going, "what receives measured, gets managed." how can you control your money without understanding what you earn each month? If you don't have a full concrete variety, decide your month-to-month profits after taxes. It may be less complicated if you're a salaried worker with a regular paycheck. Freelancers might also need to estimate their monthly earnings.

As soon as you have got quite a number, upload in any extra side gig money. Maybe you babysit sporadically or have a weblog that earns ad revenue; otherwise, you educate a weekly health elegance. Anything higher profits you win, add it into your monthly take-domestic pay.

3. Music wherein You Spend Your money

Pull out your credit card statements, housing, and utility payments. Financial institution statements consisting of ATM withdrawals, and any digital fee facts, together with Venmo or PayPal. Both open a spreadsheet or get out old fashioned paper and pen – it's time to overall your fees.

It helps to categorize as you parse your spending. For example, you may label purchases as wishes, wishes, or savings/debt. Or, you could get extra particular and add classes, including leisure, meal prices, travel, and transportation. It's as much as you how lots inside the weeds you want to get.

After you bring together charges into one spot, total each class to peer wherein the bulk of your money is going. You are probably surprised at how an awful lot you spend ingesting out.

4. Have a Plan – Any Plan

Now that you realize how much you earn, as well as how a good deal you spend, it's time to make a plan. The best financial plans align your precedence (money management tip No. 1) with your spending behavior.

Permit's say you're a health buff. While you totaled your fees, you determined that during a median month, you put money into a gym club, yoga magnificence card, and new athletic tools. If that's crucial to you, you won't reduce it out. But, to meet something priority you've set — let's say it's an emergency fund — you'll need to cut prices somewhere else. That could suggest shopping at a reduction grocery store or brown-bagging your lunch rather than ordering takeout along with your coworkers.

Whether or not you pay for a finances program like YNAB, or select a simple Excel spreadsheet, that's as much as you. It brings us to cash management tip No. 5...

5. Keep on with the Plan

After you choose a plan, supply it a try for as a minimum a month. You want that lengthy to peer if it works for you. Something much less, and you received see the gain of maintaining a watch for your finances.

So find finances you want to try, get began, and live with it. It's that simple. In case you want, Washington recommends you "surround yourself with visible representations" of your desires. So if you're saving to your subsequent global journey, you could place up pictures of your dream trip to maintain your purpose clean on your thoughts.

6. Count on Emergencies

Cash management guidelines

No matter what your precedence is, you'll want to have a few readily available liquid budget.

Maybe you're specializing in paying down your scholar loans, and you're no longer involved with building a hefty emergency fund. That's quality, and you don't indeed should keep six months of expenses. However, you have to shop for at least 3.

You in no way realize what may happen. You or a companion should lose a task, or have a medical emergency or any quantity of circumstances. Whether you want it or no longer, life occurs.

Having cash to deal with troubles as they arrive up will help you experience more comfortable and a bit extra organized. Most emergencies add sufficient stress as it is. Put off an element of worry with an economic cushion.

The way you placed money away for emergencies is as much as you. Maybe you funnel all of your facet gig money to an account you only contact in an absolute emergency. Or, it's in which any birthday or any immediate cash goes. It can be as easy as a small, month-to-month car-deposit. It's up to you.

7.   Store   Early   and   frequently

It rule holds genuine irrespective of your present-day priority. The earlier you shop, the sooner you may build interest. You don't even want an investment account to begin income interest. Maximum of the tremendous financial savings debts generate interest, and people bills are FDIC insured. Meaning you don't have the hazard of losing your money, as with a brokerage account.

It rule also applies to retirement. The sooner you start setting cash away in an IRA or 401(k), the higher. Even if you're years faraway from retiring, you continue to need to don't forget the future. Your money stands to grow the maximum in case you begin as quickly as feasible.

8. Take advantage of loose money

You don't want to overlook what property is to be to you. If your business enterprise gives 401(ok) matching, you must take gain of the advantage. It's unfastened cash.

Any other location to look at is your medical health insurance plan. Perhaps your process gives a reduced gymnasium club. Take gain of all of the advantages your activity offers; you might keep some critical coins.

9. Relook Your Debt

Take a look at your total debt (cash management tip No. 2). Is there something you can refinance for a decrease charge? Perhaps it's moving a balance to a credit card with decrease interest. Or, it's consolidating student loans. It's worth combing through your debt with a first-rate enamel comb to look if you may find a way to shop.

10. Find What Works – And hold Doing It

Another commonplace maxim that applies to money control is "if it's not broke, don't fix it." once you discover a system that works, don't get distracted by new apps or conflicting financial advice.

It's tempting to strive the following beautiful issue, mainly if it guarantees to be less complicated, less complicated, or quicker. But, if you're in a rhythm that works — you're saving money, meeting financial desires and constructing protection — preserve chugging alongside. Your focus will pay off.

How are you going to be smart with your cash?

In case you need to make cash over the long haul, picking investments isn't the actual problem. While research compares how well investments perform to how nicely investors carry out, there's continually a gap. Traders almost forever do worse than the investments do.

The studies typically examine traders' real returns in stock budget to the joint replacements of the budget themselves. To be clear, they're seeking to evaluate the returns buyers get to the returns investments get. Is there, in reality, a distinction? Oh, you guess there may be. Typically, the studies find that the returns buyers have earned over time are a whole lot lower than the returns of the joint investment.

So what's occurring? The trouble is our behavior. We do dumb such things as shopping for excessive and promoting low or selecting a stock that gives you a stable go back — at the same time as paying twice that during hobby on credit card debt. And if we hold to do dumb matters, it doesn't remember what the funding is; we'll screw it up.

A lot of financial recommendation is straightforward and easy ("earn greater, spend less.") however so is maximum dieting recommendation ("eat less, exercise extra") and we don't do it. It's easy — yet now not accessible.

So who can lead us out of It trap? Carl Richards writes about private finance for the New York Times and is the bestselling author of the behavior hole and the only-web page monetary Plan.

He places it entirely without a doubt: "monetary achievement is greater approximately behavior than it's miles approximately talent."
Reminder: You cannot predict the future
There may be no "best" funding. Timing is always a problem. Human beings stated internet stocks keep going up — after which 2000 happened. Buying a home becomes a surefire bet — and then 2008 rolled around.

Trying to pick out an inventory's destiny boom path based on past growth is like looking to guess if a coin will come up heads or tails while you know that the last toss becomes ahead. The previous toss tells you not anything.

Smarter-with-cash

Some human beings will argue: "however Apple climbed extra than four, 000 percent from the quilt of 2000 to the give up of 2010!" certain, however, do you think it's going to maintain doing that for all time? Of course not. So we're returned to predicting the destiny. And, unluckily, your Magic eight Ball keeps announcing, "reply hazy, try once more."

It shouldn't paralyze you. You're going to make investments your cash someplace. But you want to base your decisions on sound ideas — now not assumed continually uncertain consequences.

To enhance your price range over the lengthy haul, you need a plan. No, it doesn't should be a few 200-page behemoth you'll by no means ever take a look at and doesn't require you to research every cable and phone bill you acquired during the last 15 years.

The plan can suit on an index card
Ask, "What Does money mean To Me?"
Economic making plans appear so overwhelming that our first reaction is to throw up our fingers and beg any expert to "just inform me what to do." but that doesn't paintings.

Carl requested pinnacle economic managers to advise him as though he changed into a new customer — however; he wouldn't let them ask him any questions. They just needed to make blind guidelines. And exactly zero of them should responsibly do it.

Financial selections almost always are lifestyle choices. Before you decide on your business desires, you want to choose your lifestyle goals. When you hyperlink monetary selections to life decisions, you come upon a unique set of demanding situations. Absolutely everyone's economic state of affairs turns into precise, due to the fact their goals are individual. It's not about abstractions like a relaxed retirement or a university education—it's about your vision of departure and your baby's training. What brings you happiness may not convey your neighbor's delight—and a canned plan gained painting for both considered one of you.

And so the primary — and most essential — question to invite your self is, "What does money imply to me?" (Yeah, I know, you didn't anticipate economic making plans to sound like you're speaking to a therapist.)

Your project doesn't want to be crystal clear, and it may alternate. However, you'll need it as a North superstar, so you don't go chasing every "subsequent big issue" you examine about inside the newspaper or the new inventory Uncle Jack mentions at the vacation dinner desk.

When you have a partner or companion, you'll need to have It dialogue together because their North big name might be one of a kind than yours.

Smarter-with-money

Once you've got a concept of what cash approach to you, you want to be extra concrete about your desires. Specify three large ones. Do you want to be all set for retirement 30 years from now? Or to put your children through university in 15? Do you want to shop for a house in five years? Or journey extra in 2?

Carl says the technique is ready figuring out wherein you want to go, where you are now, and then narrowing the distance. Due to the fact the number one query when evaluating any investment is, "Will It help me reach my dreams?"

And now which you know what's essential, we can speak about conduct. And conduct often comes right down to emotions.

Emotions can be the most critical matters in our lives. Emotions could make recollections that final if you're no longer careful.

Feelings can be Very expensive

We purchase high and promote low due to the fact we feel safe when we comply with the %. We preserve directly to our organization's inventory even if it's no longer aligned with our desires as we think unswerving.

And we exchange shares unnecessarily as it feels, rightly a laugh. There's a phrase for that: playing.

What are we able to all agree on approximately playing? It's fun, exciting, and something you'll in no way advise every person use as the idea for their retirement or their youngsters' schooling.

Investing is not enjoyable. Base your choices on dreams and concepts, not for your feelings approximately what's going to happen. Don't "play" the inventory marketplace; that's how you get performed.

But right now, you can no longer have lots of coins to even think about investing. So what's a useless-easy manner to start spending much less?

Use the 72-Hour check

Manifestly, you need to do what each financial advice column since the sunrise of time recommends: tune your spending. It's dull — but as we found out, slow is ideal. Spending much less is crucial — but it's not smooth. How are we able to make it a bit easier?

Luckily, Jeff Bezos created a terrific feature that will help you manage your spending. It's called your Amazon purchasing Cart. Face it; very few of the belongings you buy online need to know without delay. Any further, something you will have offered with one-click on goes to your purchasing Cart for a mandatory 72-hour preserving pattern.

After three days, when the gimme-gimme-gimme emotions have died down, objectively ask if It issue is more important than getting closer to the dreams for your one-web page financial plan.

After I go back to the site, I rarely experience as strongly about shopping for what's in my cart. So I delete the ones items and inside the process store myself quite a few cash and the need to discover more space. The best issue approximately the seventy-two-hour take a look at is that very few things ought to be correctly sale now. The more significant time gives a cushion: we're no longer announcing "no"; we're genuinely no longer giving in to our urge for instant gratification.

Automate desirable conduct

The easiest way to not make dumb decisions is to allow now not yourself virtually make the selections. Most, if promptly, not all, online financial sites assist you in automating transactions.

Let your Dr. Jekyll set up transfers to savings, bills of bills, and whatever else vital so your Mr. Hyde doesn't pass on a spending spree.

Instead of forcing yourself to make those decisions again and again, make them computerized so your exact intentions can change into proper conduct. You may automate your savings and your 401(k) allocations and ensure they automatically rebalance, and I additionally advocate automating positive set bills, like mortgages or vehicle loans. The point is: using making those choices automated; the temptation to cheat will lower.

You're spending a touch much less and painlessly saving higher. Now how do you accurately compare the ones investments that accepted lengthy earlier than you examine that insanely useful weblog put up on personal finance?

Use in a single day take a look at

You're now a lot greater clarity to your financial goals. But you weren't earlier than while to procure the investments you're presently maintaining. How do you get the whole thing in alignment?

Ask yourself what you would do if someone got here in and offered all of your investments in a single day. The next morning you wake up, and you left with a hundred percent cash for your account. Here's the take a look at you may repurchase the same investments at no cost. Could you construct a balanced portfolio? If not, what modifications could you make? Why aren't you making them now?

Your present-day investments at the moment are associated with your desires. So how do you begin making new, suitable investments?

Recognize The fundamental policies Of investing

No 1: Pay down debt.

Wide variety 2: Are you sure you couldn't pay down other debt?

In case you're maintaining on to debt with high-interest rates, paying the ones money owed down trumps pretty much some other financial investment you could make folks that apprehend interest earn it.

Think about it: paying off debt has an assured go back — 0 chances. You don't pay interest on what you don't owe. And debt always stands in the manner of pursuing those dreams you just defined.

Number 3: make sure to diversify. By way of no longer placing all of your eggs in one basket, you reduce the chance and often boom returns.

The magic of diversification is that you could take man or woman investments, which, when viewed in isolation, are, in my opinion, unstable, and blend them in a portfolio. Doing so creates funding that's certainly much less risky than the man or woman additives and regularly comes with a more return. In finance, It is as near as we get to a free lunch.

In finance, "unsystematic danger" is having a bet on a particular stock, quarter, or enterprise. It requires understanding the destiny. We need to take away unsystematic chance. We need to focus on "systematic danger." which means making a bet at the machine as a whole.

What you want as a substitute is to tackle "systematic hazard"—It indicates you invested within the idea of capitalism as a whole. It is base on the idea that no matter the up-and-down nature of the marketplace (and the way terrifying the "downs" are), over lengthy durations of time, it will keep growing. Consequently, you need to own masses of shares throughout the market; positive, some of the organizations you own will fail; however, it gained without a doubt affect you due to the fact you spread your risk throughout an entire bunch.

It means a mutual budget is generally higher than person stocks. But what's the trouble with the joint price range? Expenses. You want to hold prices as little as feasible.

Lots of research has tried to tease out what makes one mutual fund higher than some other. What becomes the best predictive variable they found that determined which traders made extra cash?

It turns out that there's no longer a single variable that will help you identify how a mutual fund will perform—besides one. Price. It honestly boils all the way down to simple math: the higher you pay on your investments, the much less cash you'll grow to be retaining.

Beyond that, always evaluate your one-web page economic plan and ask if the investment helps you meet your dreams. Does it? That's interesting! However, we now realize not to agree with exhilaration. It sounds an excessive amount of like a laugh, and a smile is risky when investing.

So have a pal or member of the family ask you three inquiries to make sure you're not making a mistake:

If I make It transformation and I am right, what impact will it have on my existence?

What impact will it have if I'm wrong?

Have I been incorrect before?

If the solutions are "little," "horrendous," and "regularly," you can want to don't forget a safer funding like, say, Russian roulette.

Be Ignorant and Lazy

A massive mistake humans make is studying an excessive amount of brief-time period economic news that leaves them itchy to buy, sell, or otherwise gamble. Say it with me now: you may expect the destiny. And neither can the specialists.

However, they want to make predictions each day, though. It has the result of assisting them in keeping their jobs and helping you lose cash. The click doesn't write testimonies about folks that stored their pennies, paid off their credit score cards, and made safe, boring investments over thirty years. (Yawn.)

So do your homework earlier after which forgets about the information. Each day updates make you irritating, and anxiety does not often result in smart money selections. Only pay attention to what sincerely subjects on your dreams and what you can manipulate. As Carl likes to say, "attention to your private economy and prevent stressful about the global one."

A few human beings will push back: "however, what approximately Black Swans! If humans had paid attention, we could have averted the 2008 disaster!" well, they've accomplished studies at the specialists who effectively predict intense shifts. And bet what?

How do you finance your cash the 50 20 30 rule?

You have reviewed your spending and created a price range, and now you know precisely how a great deal you spend on your private home, your car, discretionary spending, and what sort of you divert on your retirement bills. It is all good, but ensures you've also idea approximately the way to allocate your financial savings for things which include an emergency fund. How does your financial allocation evaluate to the quantity you have to spend and keep ideally?

Harvard financial disaster professional Elizabeth Warren—U.S. Senator from Massachusetts and named by way of TIME magazine as one of the one hundred maximum Influential people inside the world in 2010— coined the "50/30/20 rule" for spending and saving together with her daughter, Amelia Warren Tyagi.1 They co-authored an e-book on it in 2005, referred to as "all of your well worth: The closing Lifetime cash Plan."

So how do the 50/30/20 plan paintings? Right here's how Warren and Tyagi endorse you arranging your price range.

The first step: Calculate Your After-Tax profits

Your after-tax income is what remains of your paycheck after taxes are taken out, such as country tax, local tax, income tax, Medicare, and Social safety. In case you're a worker with a regular paycheck, your after-tax profits should be clean to parent out in case you take a look at your paystubs. If health care, retirement contributions, or some other deductions are complete out of your paycheck, upload them lower back in.

In case you're self-employed, your after-tax earnings equals your gross profits minus your enterprise fees, which include the price of your laptop or airfare to conferences, in addition to the amount you put apart for taxes. You are accountable for remitting your own quarterly estimated tax payments to the government due to the fact you do not have an organization to take care of it for you.2

Keep in mind that being a self-employed approach that you must additionally pay the self-employment tax, so encompass It in your calculations. The self-employment tax is double what you will pay in Medicare and Social security taxes if you were employed.

Step: restriction your needs to 50% of Your After-Tax earnings

Now cross returned for your finances, and figure out how plenty you spend on "wishes" every month—things like groceries, housing, utilities, health insurance, vehicle bills, and automobile coverage. According to Warren and Tyagi and their 50/30/20 rule, the quantity which you spend on these items needs to general no more than 50% of your after-tax pay.3

Of direction, now you need to differentiate among which expenses are "needs" and that are "wishes." basically, any payment that you could forgo with the simplest minor inconveniences. It will consist of your cable bill or back-to-school garb. Any fee that could seriously affect your best of existence, consisting of power and prescription drugs, is a want.

If you can't forgo a charge such as the least payment on a credit score card, it could be taken into consideration a "need," because your credit score could be negatively impacte if you don't pay the minimum. Via the same token, if the minimum charge required is $25 and you frequently pay $one hundred a month to preserve plausible stability, that extra $ seventy-five isn't always a want.

Step 3: restrict your "wishes" to 30%

It sounds fantastic at the surface. If you could put 30% of your cash toward your needs, you'll be thinking about lovely footwear, an experience of Bali, salon haircuts, and Italian eating places.

No longer so speedy—your "needs" do not consist of extravagances. They include the primary niceties of existence that you revel in, like that limitless text messaging plan, your house's cable invoice, and cosmetic (now not mechanical) maintenance for your car.

Step four: Spend 20% on savings and debt repayments

Now about the extra $ seventy-five, you pay on that credit score card every month. It truly is neither a need nor a need. It is the "20" in the 50/30/20 rule. It's in a class all its personal.

You ought to spend at least 20% of your after-tax profits repaying money owed and saving money for your emergency fund and your retirement accounts. Three if you deliver credit score card stability, the minimum price is a "want," and it counts toward 50%. Anything more is an extra debt compensation, which is going closer to It 20% class. In case you deliver a mortgage or a vehicle loan, the minimum fee is a "want," and any higher bills depend closer to "financial savings and debt repayment."

An example of the 50/30/20 Plan

Shall we embrace your total take-domestic pay each month is $three,500. The usage of the 50-30-20 rule, you may spend no more than $1,750 on your wishes according to month. You probably can't manage to pay for a $1,500-a-month hire or loan price, at the least no longer until your utilities, car payment, minimum credit card bills, insurance premiums, and other requirements of lifestyles do not exceed $250 a month.

If you already personal your own home or you locked into a rent, you are quite a lot caught with that $1,500 payment. Take into account relocating while your lease expires to make your price range more achievable or test your other "wishes" to look if there is a manner that you can lessen any of them. Maybe store for extra low-priced insurance or switch the stability on that credit score card to 1 with a lower interest rate, so your minimum payment drops a bit.

You intend to be able to healthy some of these prices into 50% of your take-home after-tax income.

You may spend $1,050 a month to your "wishes" based totally on that $three, 500 you're bringing home every month. You might don't forget doing without some matters and shifting some of It money in your "needs" column if you're developing quick there—now not necessarily indefinitely, however, till you could get your desires down to a higher potential degree. Take into account, and you continue to want 20% leftover so you can shop and pay down your money owed according to the 50/30/20 plan.

Now you have got $seven-hundred left, that final 20%. You realize what to do with it. Pay down on debt, keep for an emergency, and plan to your future.

How do you Spend accurately?

Frugal residing doesn't must be lifestyles without fun. In truth, you might be surprised how smooth it is to trim your costs with a little persistence and to make plans. The more you could get out of every dollar you spend, the more money you will shop for ability emergencies, a college training for your children, vacations to exclusive locations, or anything large ticket object your coronary heart desires. To get you commenced, here are seven ways to spend money wisely.

1. Pony up for exceptional where it counts.

The most inexpensive choice isn't continually the satisfactory choice. What's the point of purchasing a cheap pair of shoes if they're going to end up worn out and rugged inside a few months? It'd be more reasonable to pay $50 for an outfit an excellent way to be in final form subsequent 12 months than $20 for an outfit that has to get replaced in much less than six months.

2. Purchase everyday label groceries.

You would be difficult-pressed to locate any difference among name-logo and regularly occurring labels inside the grocery store. Don't accept as real with me? Snatch a bottle of a name-emblem peanut butter and the established grocery store range and compare the ingredients. Repeat It exercise with things like canned vegetables, bins of pasta, cleaning merchandise, and medicine. While you purchase name-brands, you are not deciding to buy the product itself, but rather the concept in the back of the product. In other phrases: name manufacturers are extra pricey due to the fact they've higher advertising budgets (no longer better first-rate).

3. Cut down on meals waste. Answer absolutely: if you had to guess, how many of the groceries you buy become uneaten and tossed inside the trash? In step with a study by way of the natural resources protection middle, the joint American own family of 4 throws away almost 50% of the meals they buy, ensuing in an annual loss as much as $2,275. To avoid grocery waste, exchange your thinking about purchasing. Instead of creating a list of gadgets to buy without thought procedure, plan by using writing down a weekly agenda of the unique meals you'll cook earlier than you go to the shop. If it is not mandatory within the components you want, it doesn't move in your cart. Make observe of the way lots of meals receives tossed in the trash and reduce the amount you buy It. If you'd want to shop time and money, take a look at out. Its critical aid on as soon as a month cooking.

4. Look ahead to it

Retail remedy is nearly continually a terrific idea; however, smart customers understand how to be affected person. Why need to you spend $one hundred on that fantastic skirt now if it's going to be marked right down to make room for fall and winter clothes? Be affected person, and you may be reward with a steep charge reduction. Keep an eye fixed out for the unique gives that you may refuse.

5. Clip coupons for special occasions.

Eating out is considered one of my favorite date night activities; however, it sure can empty a wallet rapidly. Eating places are commonly generous with their offers, so begin clipping for serious cash savings. Want to make coupon-clipping a fun and exciting sport?

Do It.

6. Visit the movie.

Overdue night movies are so excited. Why could you pay double the matinee ticket rate just for the pleasure of fighting a far more massive crowd and suffering to find a seat in a packed auditorium? Go to the new display to store some dough and beat the gang.

7. Hit up the thrift saves.

Consignment shops are full of offers on barely-used garb that might save you heaps of money for your wardrobe. If you have in no way taken into consideration thrift buying because you're afraid the great won't be up-to-par, deliver it a risk. The thrift stores in my neighborhood are pretty picky about the gadgets they accept, so I guess you are probably surprised.

CHAPTER 4
HOW CAN YOU SPEND LESS AND SAVE MORE

Did your list of recent 12 months' resolutions encompass financial goals? If so, through March, you're new spending, and saving behavior should begin to feel habitual, in step with one have a look at that determined it takes 66 days, on common, to form a brand new dependency.

However, that doesn't mean your new frugal way of life has ended up easy or enjoyable. It may be tough to cognizance to your budget all the time, especially when the maximum of your goals – which include sending your youngsters to university or saving for retirement – seems a long way off.

1. Store cash on eating out

You're consuming at home extra frequently and diverting loads of greenbacks once spent at eating places every month in the direction of debt compensation and other monetary goals. Congratulations! It's feasible to reward yourself with the occasional night out without breaking your budget. Break up an entrée or eat an appetizer as your main dish. If you have a family, look for "youngsters consume free" nights. Drink water as your beverage at the eating place, and revel in a pleasant glass of wine or craft beer at home earlier than or after dining out.

Some other a laugh manner to dine out on-the-cheap are food vans. They provide an extensive type of exquisite cuisines at a fraction of the price of conventional restaurants. Plus, you could dine al fresco and take in the points of interest and sounds of the local community.

2. Search for unfastened sports

Many towns offer a bunch of free activities, mainly in the summer season months. Use social media equipment and the web to discover listings for network sports and make your date night a little less expensive.

3. Create a game or task around your saving dreams

Pick out a person who's additionally running closer to private finance goals – a sibling, best buddy, or co-employee – and mission them to a save-off. The person that saves the most money over the next month (or more) wins the sport. Make the prize something less expensive, such as the loser doing some carrier for the winner. Assume washing the winner's automobile or cooking them a self-made meal. But, there is no loser's right here if you're each saving cash! Click on right here for different fun and competitive approaches to keep.

4. Store storage sales

Another LifeHack.Org concept: "as a substitute for purchasing new fixtures, go searching at nearby storage income to peer if you could discover something that works. It might just want a little refinishing. It could turn into a fun assignment and prevent money as well."

5. Make biweekly payments

Trendy loans and credit score cards require one price every month. A biweekly method divides It month-to-month fee in half and will pay that amount every two weeks. Due to the fact, there are 52 weeks in a year; you're making 26 biweekly bills (the equal of 13 month-to-month payments). On a monthly foundation, the charge quantity is identical. However, a further month's charge every 12 months can reduce interest costs and shorten the time of a loan.

Ways to spend less and keep extra money

1. Pay yourself First

What is left of their financial institution account at the end of the month over to their savings account.

But the fact is: That isn't always a first-rate manner to keep cash.

So it's a far better concept to invest in your savings account right once you have been pleased instead.

Pay your credit card invoice, your rent, and any other payments which you might have after which transfer something percent of your income you've got decided on into your savings account.

Need to spend less and shop for money?

Do your splurging once you pay your bills and placed away cash for yourself on your financial savings account.

2. Trade the manner you exercise

Quite a few humans have gym memberships that they don't use, or that they don't make the most.

Sit down and determine out precisely how a great deal of money each trip to the health club is costing you. It can be extra than you recognize.

If the health club does not feel worth it, it could be time to alternate your exercise habitual.

A brilliant way to do It is by using getting outdoor! Trekking is an exquisite manner to get some cardio in. And it's also a super manner to explore your neighborhood place and spend some time with friends, family – or canine. Just make sure you get a few sturdy on foot footwear, so you don't get injured.

If you want to boom your center power and enhance your flexibility, you could strive out little yoga at home. Yoga with Adrienne is one of the maximum famous YouTube yoga channels. She provides extraordinary styles of yoga — depending on what a part of your body is sore.

Need to spend less and keep greater?
Attempt swimming! Pools are a little less pricey than gyms. And swimming is a splendid way to get a whole-body workout — without setting any strain to your joints or exacerbating any antique accidents.

3. Discover ways to Meal Plan
All of us stay busy existence. As a result, you may be spending a bit extra coins than you would like on takeout and going out to eat.

The best manner to shop that money is to learn how to meal plans.

Suppose through the coming week and your commitments on every night. Afterward, exercise sessions what the best meal could be.

While you move grocery store purchasing, convey a clear list of what you need. After all, you don't want to become getting domestic with full-size portions of food which you won't sincerely come to be consuming.

It's also a good idea to start batch cooking on weekends. If you do, then you may take lunch to paintings somewhat of buying it. Plus, you can create balanced and attractive food for yourself if you spend a day cooking.

If that doesn't mean attraction to you, you may always take leftovers to work. Or slap together a smooth, less expensive sandwich or salad.

Need to spend less and save money?

Take your espresso with you – alternatively of buying a costly drink from your local espresso keep or Starbucks. It is additionally better for the surroundings – as you'll end up the use of far fewer takeaway cups.

4. Alternate your financial institution Account

When the majority open financial institution money owed, they right now forget approximately it. Their bank account is a depository for their paycheck, and that's it.
However, it's crucial to make sure that you live clued in to what's happening at your bank. Study whether any accounts could come up with better advantages or better interest costs that you can switch.

For example, ...It financial institution of the United States evaluation suggests extraordinary aspects of that bank – which may additionally or may not attraction to you.

Want to spend much less and shop greater?
Do your research right into a bank's benefits. But if the studies baffle you, pass in and talk for the financial institution that allows you to propose what the satisfactory account is for you.

5. Check Out Your Neighborhood Library
If you may come up with the money for to guide your nearby indie book shop, go to your library instead. You may borrow unlimited books. Or you may attend free classes. Plus, you could take your children to tale time sessions with exceptional librarians who may be able to recommend you approximately what books your kids may experience.

But if you see an eBook, you believe you studied is brilliant, sense free to make investments. Investing you're getting to know and growth ought to be a priority.

6. Use much less energy At home

At home, a neat way to shop the planet and store your money at an equal time is to use much less electricity. The perfect manner of doing that is to interchange the lighting each time you leave a room.

However, remember that you must also transfer off any appliances like your TV that may have left on standby. Your TV makes use of nearly as lots of strength as watching it'd use.

Need to spend less and save more?

Transfer to energy-efficient mild bulbs – they last for longer, meaning which you'll replace them much less often, and also they use drastically much less strength.

7. Trade how you use your vehicle

While it comes to move, remember how a whole lot you need your vehicle. Now not best are they costly to run. However, car insurance also can be extremely highly-priced.

If you stay in a metropolis, you will be capable to stroll more regularly or take public transport, and both of these things are an awful lot better for the surroundings than using your car all the time.

In case you need a car, why no longer keep in mind shopping for a used car rather than a modern one? Ultra-modern automobiles move down in fee extraordinarily speedy, and they require you to extend coverage payments, so that you may additionally surely be losing cash if you pass for one.

Want to spend less and store cash?

A used automobile might most effectively be 12 months or so antique, but it will likely be lots inexpensive each to shop for and to run.

8. Use your playing cards differently

An excellent manner of storing cash is to start the usage of your credit score cards much less. It's suitable to use them strategically. Many people use their cards to deal with debt.

For instance, if you don't have a good deal cash within the bank – and you need to pay on your puppy's medication – a credit card is an excellent way to do It.

However, it's essential to make sure that you earn as a minimum the minimum price each month. And that you don't permit the interest mount up an excessive amount.

Paying your credit score card invoice can grow your credit rating – and be appropriate for you within a long time.

Need to spend less and save money?
In case you find yourself making too many thoughtless purchases to your card, it's time to go for cash instead!

Examine your weekly finances and depart your cards at home, earning money out of the financial institution as an alternative and paying simplest with that.

Recall: it is going to be lots simpler when you could sincerely bodily see what you're spending.

9. Deal with Your feelings

Spend much less and store cash with meditation. There are quite a few human beings out there who use spending money as a manner to feel better. If you feel blue, you go online and blow some cash on some new garments.

You go to a make-up store and buy some products which you don't need, even though you're flawlessly glad with the ones that you have already got.

Many humans use buying matters as a way to get a spike of euphoria to keep away from feelings of disappointment or boredom.

How Can You Convince Yourself to Save More

Saving cash is not something that comes obviously to the general public. In reality, research has shown human beings with much less money tend to have a more robust time making economic and time control-related choices.

In quick, the psychological elements concerned with saving cash matter — plenty. So it might appear like a reasonably daunting venture to hold your bank account above water so you can pay bills and cowl the essential month-to-month expenses. The best news is that even while you're in a situation like It, there are a few things you may do to pressure yourself to shop and boom your coins drift.

1. Determine out what your Discretionary actual income is

In case you take a seat down and upload up all your monthly fees, then subtract that out of your month-to-month take-domestic pay, you might be surprised at how lots discretionary earnings you have. The general public doesn't even do the math, so it just seems like things are tight, when in reality, they have loads of extra money that they're just now not coping with nicely. (See also: cash control in five mins an afternoon)

Map it all out so that you know what has to go out on a month-to-month foundation, and then deliver your satisfactory wager for things that vary like gas and groceries. If the cash leftover is round $four hundred, then you could probably effectively take at least 1/2 of that and positioned it away. If it is $2 hundred, then $one hundred every week can move into financial savings.

2. Recognize That It doesn't Take tons

Lots of humans are beneath the effect that "saving cash" means placing aside a high percentage of their weekly pay, which usually is not something they could manage to pay. That notion on my own is sufficient to frustrate a person to stray into a mindset of "since I can't shop loads, I just might not shop any in any respect."

Before you pass into a savings plan, understand that saving money is frequently merely one small step at a time. Economic advisors will let you know that the sooner you start saving for retirement, the much less you need to put away every week. Someone of their mid-20s who starts putting $25 each week into an investment account can count on being close to (if now not over) the $six hundred,000 mark by the time they're ready to retire.

If you could begin at age 25 and manage $57 every week (or $3,000 in step with year for ten years) in a retirement account with eight% go back, that cash might grow to over $470,000 by the point you are 65, without you having to contribute something when you're 35 years old.

The longer you wait, the more significant that weekly range receives, and the much less time your money has to grow. It could nonetheless end; however, the stress gets better. The key is to get commenced as quickly as viable, irrespective of how small the quantity you need to contribute.

3. Cut prices somewhere and placed the savings Away

You don't necessarily need to reduce into the excess income that you already revel in; as a substitute, find an area where you can cut costs. A reasonably regular recommendation is espresso, so instead of getting coffee four times a week, get it as soon as. Higher yet, make it at home for approximately 10 cents consistent with cup.

In case you skip out on coffee four times a week, it is everywhere from $15-$20 according to week. Downgrade your gym club (cut out tanning, pool, anything), and you have got maybe another $10 per week to add to the pile.

Shall we embrace conservatively that, usual, you could cut $25 out of every week. If you could put that away, there is your weekly retirement financial savings.

4. Set up automated financial savings

Nearly all online banking systems have capabilities that allow you to installation automatic transfers to ship a certain amount of cash each week from one account to every other. In It situation, it'd be sending money out of your bank account to your savings account. Or, sign on for a provider like Saved Plus, to automatically redirect a percentage of the whole thing you spend right into a savings account.

It's a perfect factor to install place after which neglect approximately for several months. If you can swing $25 according to week (and you likely can!), you will have upwards of $six hundred stored through the stop of six months.

If you could find the money for more in keeping with week, and you are comfortable sending it over to savings, the better that weekly number is, the better. Keep in mind that it would not need to be excessive. You may even do $15 if that's higher potential. It will all rely on your price range.

5. Make contributions extra on your 401(okay)
If your organization offers a 401(okay) retirement plan, you will be able to provide either a percentage or dollar quantity that they take out of every test. Many employers will in shape up to 8 rate, so in case you're able to do without that money, a matched 401(k) is an excellent location for it. Plus, it'll pressure you to attend to take it out till retirement age.

Even in case you don't forget a smaller percent, it adds up towering over the years, so set a quantity and forget about which you also make that money. In some years, you may be impressed with how lots you've saved.

6. Live Busy at home

On a more practical be aware, the more time you're at home, the less of an opportunity you may exit and spend money that does not need to be pleased. It would not suggest that you have to lock yourself away and avoid going out. Still, if you could locate useful and engaging things to do at domestic, you'll in all likelihood have extra cash for your pocket on the give up of every week that can be socked away into your savings account.

Take, as an example, eating places. There are few matters on It existence that drain money from our wallets, like deciding to buy eating place food. Sure, it's amusing and entirely quality for do once in a while; but do not get into the dependency of continually relying on eating places to your food because the price (in comparison to cooking at home) is high. Attempt to consume most of your meals in your home and permit for the occasional splurge with pals or family.

7. Begin using personal Finance software program

Applications like Quicken generally cost a good bit of money, but Mint.Com is free and merely works equally. Maintaining the song of your price range as you pass can assist in preserving your checkbook balanced, and it can additionally motivate you to keep cash and put a few away at the give up of the week. The bottom line is that when you have to watch your cash exit, you will be greater careful with it as it's coming in.

8. Pay off Your Credit Card

If you've been carrying a balance in your credit card, now could be the time to pay it down and cast off your monthly fee. Now not only will the month-to-month price be off the desk, but the hobby you're paying on what you could be an aspect of the past as nicely. If you can manage to pay for to, pay it all off without delay and depart the credit score card by myself until it is an emergency.

In case you're capable of trying It, you may store cash every month with the aid of default, actually because you don't need to worry approximately the ones payments. Take that sum (something it is probably) and placed it in a short or long term financial savings account.

9. Artificially reduce Your Paycheck

We generally tend to live close to the ceiling of anything we make, staying close to the most quantity of spending that our income can take care of.

10. Drink one much less Beer and Pocket the savings

If you exit for a drink a few times per week and drink multiple beers, perhaps two or three, keep on with one drink and pocket the financial savings.

On the give up of the yr, take hold of your total, and position it all for your financial savings account. Two much less beers per week might be approximately $15, increased with the aid of fifty-two weeks is $780.

11. Go along with Netflix as opposed to TV

Buying television every month is about $60 on a terrific day. If you may live without it, a Netflix instant subscription is best $eight in line with month, providing you with an additional $ fifty-two. Multiply that via twelve months, and you've got every other $624 in your credit.

12. Prioritize Saving money

If you do not prioritize saving cash, it's never going to manifest. You have to make it an emotional priority and something that you're enthusiastic about to shop on a steady foundation. Without that pressure and choice to accumulate your financial savings, it will be a regular uphill battle to even stay within the black.

We begin with desirable intentions like preserving a budget. And maybe we'll download an app to tune our spending.

Top 10 approaches to live greater economically nowadays

It's too unspecific, immeasurable, and there's no concrete plan for achievement. What you want is something precise to work.

Instead, swap your savings goal with one or higher concrete frugal goals, and you'll automatically meet your financial savings goals.

Below is a list of 25 particular purpose thoughts that you would possibly need to remember. Don't attempt to do all of them. Just choose one or frequently, while we set desires or resolutions, we go all out at the beginning gate without leaving any puff for the rest of the race. We can end up overwhelmed, especially as soon as the holidays are over, and we ought to try to healthy our resolutions in with business as standard.

So as a substitute, choose one or dreams that resonate with you, create a plan and opt for it.

A PLAN TO attain YOUR FRUGAL dreams
Earlier than you get commenced, right here's what you need to do to make sure you're a hit at reaching your frugal goals.

Recognize how an awful lot you spend already at the habit you want to exchange. For instance, in case you need to lessen your grocery expenses, you have to realize how a good deal you currently spend. Set a practical goal for away a good deal you want to be spending. A goal 'range,' for example, $2 hundred – $240, is greater flexible and possible than an actual quantity.

Select one or two sustainable action steps that you can do each and each week to reduce your expenditure gradually. Maintaining with our grocery example, begin by making plans and cooking one extra vegetarian meal per week. That's it. Depending on how a whole lot you spend on meat for a meal, that could be around $15 per week financial savings or $780 a 12 months with one small habit alternate.

Once you have that addiction below your wing, choose some other sustainable action step. By sustainable, I suggest something you could without difficulty work in your modern way of life each week. By the cease of the year, you'll be saving sizeable amounts for your groceries, and you'll be plenty extra a success than if you had long past in gung-ho in January and then went again to antique spending styles in February.

12 ways TO BE FRUGAL IT NEW year

Spend With a Plan

Budgeting receives all of it backward. Don't spend and then song your expenses. Plan how you're going to spend your tough-earned money in advance of time.

Having a game plan in your cash isn't complicated. Begin with the aid of getting your banking proper. Check out the free cheat sheet on setting up your banking for saving fulfillment.

Begin a Savings Plan

The vital thing to successful saving is to pay yourself first and automate the method.

Decide on how a good deal you need to save each payday and then use online banking to switch that cash for your financial savings frequently account before you've even were given out of bed and had time to spend.

Also reading:

Making Saving cash as clean as doing not anything

Reduce Waste

Decreasing waste isn't simplest properly on your hip pocket, but it's also desirable for the surroundings. Albert Einstein is quoted as announcing "doing the equal component again and again and looking ahead to exclusive consequences is the meaning of insanity." Buying unmarried-use objects time and again, the use of them as soon as and throwing them inside the bin is an insane waste of cash.

Switch it around. Buy once and use it again and again and shop a packet load over the path of the year.

Lessen meals Waste
Cut Your Grocery invoice
Cutting your grocery invoice is one of the quickest and simplest ways to store cash.

Right here's what you want to recognize to reduce your grocery invoice and make existence less difficult:

How to consume healthy on a tight price range
The very best manner to Menu Plan
The way to Batch cooks the easy way to save time and money
The way to Stockpile the proper manner to save money

Make tap Water flavor as precise as or better than Bottled

Ideas for Brown Bagging Your Lunch to work

Closing Meal planning method

Join the Library

Your local library is seriously the excellent supply of unfastened stuff around. Now not merely books, however, borrow tracks, DVDs, TV series, audiobooks, games, puzzles, pc games, and toys. And in all likelihood, more matters I will think around. Circulate music and movies without spending a dime. Take free publications.

Purchase the whole lot at a reduction

One of the pleasant methods to keep and store is only to pay coins – it saves you from overspending and going into debt.

That doesn't mean you can by no means use plastic, but best spend if you recognize you have got sufficient coins in financial savings to pay off your card the very same day.

While you do come to buy something, make a purchasing addiction of around for the high-quality rate and haggling for a better deal.

Entertain yourself for free

There's no doubt that maximum people spend way an excessive amount of time in the front of a display screen. And with pay-tv, streaming services, gaming subscriptions, and online shopping, we surely do SPEND while we're in front of a display.

So It year, make the purpose of spending much less time and money on displays and more time exploring the free amusement in your nearby area.

Picnic inside the park, visit the beach, revel in free nearby events, go to your library. There are hundreds of things to experience free of charge that now not only leaves you with extra for your pocket; you'll be healthier as well.

DE clutter

Maximum people are drowning in an excessive amount of stuff. Clearing the decks now not only frees up extra area; however, it additionally frees up time (much less time dealing with your stuff), explains your headspace, and you may make a few extra cash promoting the things you don't want anymore.

Study a new skill

You could never have too many talents. You would possibly select to research a brand unique frugal ability, like baking or gardening, or update your professional skills. Take a look at your local library free books and online learning assets within the strength you want to research. Go to YouTube, that's a treasure trove of free getting to know. Take a free college course or a network application or an online route.

Make gifts It year

When is the excellent time to begin making Christmas presents? Proper now! It takes time to craft, so it's nice to start early. Use your newfound abilities to keep cash and make gifts with that means. You by no means know, it can come to be a hobby that makes you money on the facet as correctly.

Decrease your payments

Apart from the groceries, power fees are some other rate that could make a massive dent out of the budget, but one we have a certain amount of manipulate over. It yr, why not take steps to lower your strength intake and decrease your payments.

Transfer and keep

How to make massive financial savings for your strength invoice
Make your property more energy green with Passive solar design

Begin a lawn

Loads may be said to begin a garden. Now not handiest can it help feed your family, but it's additionally an excellent way to de-pressure and experience the outdoors. And youngsters love gardening.

You don't need some area to start a lawn; if you're new to it, it's critical to start small and paintings your way up. Some pots of herbs on the windowsill or at the front door are a great location to begin.

How to Get Out of Debt on a Low Income

Getting out of debt is hard sufficient if you have lots of cash coming in, not to mention facing It project while you're on a low income.

However, here's the component: it is possible to get out of debt on low earnings. However, wait: there's extra! It's also possible to do it without promoting foremost belongings, just like the residence or automobile you don't yet have.

Take inventory of your monetary scenario

You could repair the debt which you don't renowned you have got due to the fact one of the essential elements of any debt-reduction approach is deciding on which mortgage to address first.

As you're operating, make sure you list the amount, the interest, the term, your monthly payments, and to be had credit score restrict for every debt. It could help you understand the whole breadth of the situation, and come up with substantial numbers to work with while you create finances (spoiler alert).

And while you're at it, make separate spreadsheets to list all your other month-to-month costs—things like food, utilities, car payments, and many others.—plus one for all the cash that you have coming in from diverse assets.

281

After that, you may make finances the usage of zero-sum budgeting strategies

No one likes creating finances. However, agree with me: that is the best manner you'll manipulate to get your debt beneath manipulate.

Once all of your charges and debts, you can go through the manner of allocating your monthly income as essential. Holly Johnson is a personal finance blogger, and she once determined herself buried underneath a mountain of debt. She used 0-sum budgeting to get out.

The idea at the back of 0-sum budgeting is that at the end of the month, you don't have a single cent leftover because each greenback has given to bills, money owed, and savings. It can sound a little unsettling; however, it's going to assist you in recovering work a lot quicker.

While you create your budget, the first matters to attend to are savings and money owed. Then you may use what's leftover for the whole thing else. If you have to reduce costs someplace, it comes from such things as amusement and transportation in preference to debt-reduction or investments.

Study your most significant fees and see where you could trim fats
Once you know where you're at regarding your debts, costs, and price range, you have to take steps to shut the purse strings. You could get out of debt in case your debt continues growing. Due to the fact you may make that money from debt payments or financial savings, it'll need to come from someplace else.

Go over your budget and categorize your spending to see where you're spending an excessive amount of cash—on transportation or eating out, for instance. Then make an expenditure reduction plan. Right here are some ideas:

Buy food in bulk, especially while it's on sale
Clip coupons for everything which you purchase, from menu to clothes to toiletries and greater
Sell your automobile (if you have one) and walk or bike to paintings—if you're like most people, you spend a median of $9,000 a yr for your car
Cook dinner greater at domestic and devour out less
Cut your subscriptions for things like cable and the health club, and choose lower service programs for vital things like cell telephones and internet

Bring your daily espresso from home in preference to shopping for out

Continually buy used: take a look at thrift stores and classifieds while you want to buy something, such as garments, fixtures, motors, or even home equipment

The most straightforward manner to address your debt is to make higher than the minimum bills

We've mentioned budgets and spending and a way to stop adding on your money owed, however now it's time to get to the nitty-gritty details of debt reduction. The primary and a number of the maximum crucial matters to recognize is It: Making just the minimum fee will result in existence-lengthy debt.

The typical American has a credit card stability of approximately $9, six hundred with a fifteen percent hobby rate. Making the minimum payment each month would depart you paying off that debt for almost 12 years! In case you need to get out of debt, you must make better-than- minimum bills.

The best way to approach debt is to tackle stability at a time

Now I realize it can now not be possible so that you can make above-minimal payments on each debt each month. And don't worry—you don't have to. However, what you do have to do is pick out one debt to pay down first. Even as you're doing that, keep making minimum bills someplace else.

For instance, say you have five money owed with unique balances. To make matters clear, we'll tell the minimal on each one is $one hundred. You'd begin by preparing the minimal on 4 of these debts, however, pay, say, $200 (for a complete of $six hundred) each month towards one of the money owed till it turned into paid off.

As quickly as you cope with that first balance, you could do a happy dance and start to tackle the subsequent debt. From there, pay the minimum each month on the ultimate 3, and pay $three hundred (so that you're nonetheless paying the identical $six hundred quantity) towards the singled-out debt.

The Harvard commercial enterprise overview investigated distinctive debt discount methods. It determined that It method will let you pay off debts up to fifteen percentages quicker than in case you just spread the $six hundred lightly amongst all of the money owed.

Now the (slightly) trickier element: deciding which debts to address in which order. The first alternative is state to as the avalanche, and it involves paying the debt with the best hobby fee first.

Bruce McClary on the country full foundation for credit Counseling makes use of a ladder analogy to explain Its technique. Begin with the highest hobby account, and while that's long gone, "pass down a rung of the ladder and apply all of your greater bills to the account with the next maximum rate."

The first gain of It approach is that you'll not only pay down your debts, but you'll additionally shop extra money in the long run, way to the interest you gained pay.

Choosing a balance to address, method: The Snowball

Inside the other camp is the advocate of the snowball method. It's referred to as It due to the fact you start with the smallest debt and paintings your manner to the biggest one, like a snowball collecting velocity because it rolls down a hill.

Among a $500, a $200, and a $1,000 debt, you'd begin with the $two hundred and finish with the $1,000. It is more a mental method to debt-discount due to the fact the idea is to advantage notion and momentum out of your small preliminary successes.

The enterprise mogul Dave Ramsey devised It strategy. At the same time, as it's a sound technique, you could emerge as paying lots more hobby with It technique. But, if you have trouble staying prompted, the higher interest can be nicely really worth it to get out of debt.

Steps to getting out of debt

1. Use a balance transfer credit card

In case you are on a low income, and you are trying to get out of debt, a fantastic choice is to get a stability switch credit card. Right here's what occurs: you move the balance of 1 credit score card to a 2nd new credit scorecard, and in Its manner, you efficiently repay the perfect balance. They nearly always in my enjoy include a unique sort of advertising as an incentive for the financial institution to get your commercial enterprise. And throughout Its period, you do now not pay any interest charge in any respect, and it's an opportunity which will store money on all that interest you'll in any other case be paying at the lump sum you owe.

2. Take a debt consolidation loan

Debt consolidation is ideal for smaller or moderate amounts of debt. You can have that you are certain goes to take you higher than six months to repay.

The best information will be when you have a high credit score, and in case you do, you can pretty without difficulty get a few quite appealing prices. However, if that's no longer the case, and your credit score is lower, you'll want to be tremendously careful approximately diligently checking and evaluating, and then comparing again hobby costs.

The lowest line to take into account: with debt consolidation loans, you have to religiously take your monthly bills every month and live a hundred% dedicated to making some critical steps in being positive to stay inside your method.

Live in touch together with your creditors at some stage in the method

Consider it, or now not, creditors are humans too, and they do have an experience of sympathy.

In keeping with Bruce McCarty, "don't wait until an account is about to be closed because you've had several months of overdue or neglected bills. Inform the creditor you'd want to pay down your balance faster and want to recognize what services are to be had that will help you manipulate your debt."

The creditor can be able to reduce or cast off your hobby bills, as a minimum quickly. That is specifically genuine if you've fallen on economic difficulty these days, due to things like an activity loss or scientific emergency.

Switching to coins will help you reduce your spending

Irrespective of which technique you choose, reducing up your credit cards may additionally assist you in living on course as you hack away at your money owed.

Find a further source of income that will help you pay money owed faster

A great way of managing debts is to boom the money you have to pay them off. It isn't always a feasible option; however, there are ways you could grow your income. Here are a few thoughts to get the ball rolling:

Get an element-time job
Paintings more extra time
Promote some of your things
Hire out a part of your property
Set your sights on and work toward getting a promotion

While you start to make a touch more earnings, each extra greenback ought to pass toward your money owed. That consists of sudden income like items, tax returns, bonuses, prizes, or pay you return into

Take into account a stability switch in a few scenarios

A balance transfer can be a subtle manner to cope with debt, but there are a few conditions where it makes a sound monetary feel. One situation is that the provided should encompass a 0 percent interest fee for a fixed period. It will prevent lots of hobbies.

However, be aware that It method will work quality when you have the means to pay down a sizable amount of debt all through the 0-hobby period.

Few smart methods to pay off Debt fast

Debt can damage your financial goals. Whether you bring a small balance on your credit card every month or are staring up at a mountain of economic responsibilities, debt makes it not possible to get in advance.

1. Forestall the use of credit score playing cards

If you need to get out of debt, stop using credit cards. The more you swipe, the extra the stability climbs. Even if you continue to use your card, keep away from leaning on perks inclusive of the potential to take cash advances. As we explain in "the ten most not great credit Sins and errors":

"Unlike when you withdraw coins out of your financial institution account thru debit card, a cash increase via credit score card usually charges you a steep coins-improve price in addition to a steep interest fee. Also, hobby expenses begin collecting right away; normally from the day you are taking out the loan."

2. Pay as a lot as you could afford every month

Creating an emergency fund should be a pinnacle priority. However, as soon as you've got completed It intention, use any budget at your disposal to pay down debt. The more you play, the quicker you'll be freed from your responsibilities.

Did you store cash at the grocery save by using stacking coupons with sales? Use the savings to repay debt. Did you work a few additional times last week? Observe the more significant income for your mortgage.

3. Make cuts in your spending

Take an excellent study in which your cash is going and separate requirements from little needs. Skip daily journeys to the neighborhood espresso shop or for your favorite lunch spot. Through the years, these savings can add up. Use them to dig out of the hollow much quicker than you expected.

In case you are struggling to parent out which charges you could reduce, begin by crafting a price range. Use the software program together with You want a budget that will help you get spending priorities on target.

4. Double up on bills

Congratulations when you have paid off one credit card. But, conducting that goal doesn't suggest it's a birthday celebration time. Maintain the momentum going using allocating those budgets that are now free as much as the subsequent stability in line.

Five. Use windfalls to pay down balances

In case you get an unexpected blessing — together with a tax refund or bonus at paintings — don't spend it on a splurge. As a substitute, bite the bullet and use a portion of the budget to repay debt.

6. Freelance to earn more money

Strive your hand at freelancing to make a few greenbacks on the side. In some instances, you'll be capable of generating an enormous amount of cash, all of which should be further to the debt-payoff fund.

For some ideas on trading your abilities for cash, take a look at our "19 uncommon ways to earn extra money."

7. Address debts with the very best hobby charges first

Although some select the debt snowball technique, which indicates which you pay the money owed with the lowest balances first to construct momentum, it makes more fabulous financial experience to clean those debts with the higher hobby charges first. The ultimate purpose is to repay debt, but, so the selection is yours.

8. Don't sacrifice the matters you adore the maximum

Paying off debt might also require you to make some lifestyle adjustments; however, it doesn't should be miserable. When you have a difficult time adjusting to new occasions, put into effect gradual changes, so the method received becomes too overwhelming.

And in case you need help, take a look at our answers middle. There, you'll locate the following resources of debt-associated help:

- Credit score card debt
- Student mortgage debt
- Tax debt

How much Debt is adequate?

Some argue that any debt is an excessive amount. Others say that you have to have the best proper liability (for investing) and no awful responsibility (for spending) even though the debt is an economical device that you ought to use accurately to avoid moving into over your head.

There are numerous measures you may use to decide whether you're sporting too much debt. One we depend on is known as the full debt carrier (TDS) ratio. As a well-known guiding principle, no extra than forty% of your month-to-month gross earnings ought to move towards mortgage payments and other month-to-month debt obligations.

Realistically, the quantity of credit score you could have the funds for relies upon for your situation. If your cutting-edge employment is not cozy, you may need to tackle less credit than the advocated suggestions. However, when you have no different obligations, consisting of a mortgage, and your source of income is reliable, you may want to tackle more credit, depending on your dreams.

The right credit score level for you

Anyhow, you should borrow handiest enough money to make the purchase you have got planned, instead of borrow as lots as you may get:

Decide in your quick- and long-time period financial dreams

Calculate your average month-to-month profits and costs (consisting of all of the payments and debt you're currently paying)

Set up a saving and spending plan

The proper quantity to borrow

To discover whether or not you can have enough money to repay a loan, make the difference between your income and your fees. It is your discretionary income. Its amount, you'll want first to deduct your minimal month-to-month savings. It's an excellent concept also to deduct extra financial savings to help you meet a number of your monetary desires. These might consist of shopping for a residence or a new car or constructing an emergency fund.

What's leftover defines how tons of new credit you may have the funds to take on. If you're simplest just assembly your monthly bills, an unexpected cost could mean a severe monetary setback.

In case you are already paying off debt, which should be safe on your expense summary, you can now not be in a position to apply extra credit until your current duties are refund.

CPSIA information can be obtained
at www.ICGtesting.com
Printed in the USA
BVHW020712080521
606417BV00013B/1177

9 781802 743500